Praise for Choosing Greatness

"*CHOOSING GREATNESS* is at once deeply thoughtful and eminently practical—an excellent read for anyone looking to broaden and deepen their professional lives."

—**Daniel Pink**, #1 *New York Times* Bestselling Author of
The Power of Regret, *When*, and *To Sell Is Human*

"THIS BOOK is packed with meaningful strategies on how to identify and stay focused on the most important things. As a leader, it is critical to access the energy, attitude, and insights that will unlock new layers of growth and possibility for individuals and the organization. *Choosing Greatness* has refined techniques for all of us on how to do just that."

—**Rich DeGeronimo**, *President,*
Product and Technology, Charter Communications

"*CHOOSING GREATNESS* captures invaluable insights to accelerate your career, getting you out of your head and back into the game. It's a must-read for those in business looking to reach exceptional levels of performance."

—**Neil Blair**, *President, KPMG Corporate Finance*

"*CHOOSING GREATNESS* is a clear-eyed, evidence-based approach that gets to the heart of how to choose your future. It strips away the artifice and provides practical advice on how to achieve your goals. I worked with the ever-positive Christina and am better off for it!"

—**Jeanine Jiganti**, *General Counsel, Walmart Health & Wellness*

"DEEPLY INSIGHTFUL book and fascinating read that compels us to look at our habits and assess what's moving us forward or holding us back. Christina's evidence-based and practical approach to coaching helped transform our executive leadership team into change agents, improving our overall business growth and success!"

—**Denise Napier**, *CEO and President, Health Partners Plans*

"*CHOOSING GREATNESS* will unlock the clarity you need to be a better leader and more fulfilled at home and at work. Christina's storytelling prowess and personal experiences also make it an impossible book to put down."

—**David Cuddy**, *General Manager, Public Affairs, Microsoft*

"THIS BOOK SHOWS you how to avoid letting your habits hijack your decisions. We must make every word and action count. Our time is finite. Using this system, you can learn to focus your intensity and really light your goals on fire."

—**Wes Lujan**, *Assistant Vice President*
External Relations, Union Pacific

"CHRISTINA MAKES SENSE of the challenging topics of brain circuitry and neuroplasticity, with superb writing that lets the pages fly by! By learning to maximize good habits and break bad habits, I am convinced *Choosing Greatness* will serve an important role in helping us achieve exceptional results."

—**Dr. Adam Wolff**, *Colorado Neurological Research Center*

"*CHOOSING GREATNESS* is a catalyst for positive, professional change. Anchored in scientific findings, thought leadership, and trust-based actionable insights, Christina has created a masterclass for optimizing performance and maximizing your personal ROI. Christina's vulnerability through storytelling makes this a must-read for any professional."

—**Bill Merritt**, *Financial Services at Gartner*

"THIS BOOK is a *must-read* for those seeking to unlock their *professional potential* with practical and thoughtful advice."

—**Dan Driscoll**, *Lockheed Martin*

Choosing
GREAT NESS

Powerful Choices | Extraordinary Results

Choosing
GREAT
NESS

An Evidence-Based Approach to
Achieving Exceptional Outcomes

CHRISTINA CURTIS

Worth®

Published by Worth Books, an imprint of Forefront Books.
Distributed by Simon & Schuster.

Library of Congress Control Number: 2023901147

Print ISBN: 978-1-63763-174-4
E-book ISBN: 978-1-63763-175-1

Cover Design by Bruce Gore, Gore Studios Inc.
Interior Design by Mary Susan Oleson, BLU Design Concepts

To Steven

For all the joy you bring to the world
and the light you bring to my life.
I thought I knew what it meant to love—
and then I met you.

TABLE OF CONTENTS

AN INVITATION

....

HAVE YOU EVER FELT that there is another level of success available to you?

There is.

That you have more value to bring, more power to unlock, more growth to experience?

You do.

We are all drawn to the irresistible sensation of accomplishing great things and reaping the rewards, tangible and intangible, that come from succeeding mightily. The gun goes off and we run like hell, sprinting toward the finish line, hoping to finally reach our fullest potential, longing for that feeling of being ahead, not behind.

Instead, many of us just feel tired.

From a very young age, our lives have been framed

within a sequence of milestones. As though running through the right gates at the right time in the right way would lead to a wonderful place with endless fireworks and flashing signs saying, "You've arrived! Your fullest potential is here!"

If such a Shangri-la exists, I have yet to meet anyone who has actually been there. Instead, this illusion creates nothing more than a perpetual feeling of missing out on who we *could* have been or what we *should* have done, if only.

Having worked with Olympic athletes, world-renowned entrepreneurs, and Fortune 500 executives, I can confidently tell you that there is no race. Each of the days available to you on this planet is lined with hundreds of opportunities for your own personal victories.

Growth is the perpetual finish line.

When we focus on growth, we're consistently winning. It expands our views, enhances our insights, and sharpens our skills. Even with setbacks, we can fail with exuberance, knowing the brain is now better informed than it was before. Every lesson learned fuels our capabilities and understanding until, suddenly, we're blowing past the spot we once saw as the "finish line," with more energy in the tank and no signs of slowing down.

AN INVITATION

....

**Even with setbacks, we can fail
with exuberance, knowing
the brain is now better
informed than it was before.**

....

When we choose growth, there is always a new layer of success available, a continuous well of achievement to drink from, and unlimited possibilities to access.

Reaching your full potential is not a place; it's a *state of mind*.

NEUROSCIENCE AND
THE FOOTPRINTS OF GIANTS

Over the past two decades, I have had the honor of being an executive coach to many who have reached stratospheric levels of professional achievement. I'll be the first to admit that it can be intimidating to shake hands with these prodigiously successful people and commit to helping them reach even higher ground. Yet they do.

How?

CHOOSING GREATNESS

Exceedingly successful people have one thing in common: an innate understanding of the power of choice. They have learned that habits are best left for morning routines, grocery shopping, and workouts at the gym, where little variation is required. In key areas, however, they tolerate the discomfort that comes from choosing

....

Habits are best left for morning routines, grocery shopping, and workouts at the gym, where little variation is required.

....

growth, perpetually advancing their position and skills, as if by magic.

But it's not magic; it's science.

In between an event and our reaction to it is a space that we need to be expanding. Elbowing our way into that moment to choose the thought or action that will drive the greatest result. The challenge is, the brain is designed to conserve energy, repeating previously learned patterns to save neurological fuel. Choosing a new behavior or thought can generate discomfort, pushing us back to our old ways. But here's the thing: we can hold that discomfort and choose anyway.

And yes, we'd best admit it now: *choosing growth will sometimes feel challenging*. But *hard* is nothing more than a sensation and a mindset. After all, getting physically fit is hard, but so is being unhappy with our physical well-being. Speaking up in a meeting is hard, but so is being overlooked and unappreciated. Getting feedback is hard, but so is continuing a behavior that's holding you back. Creating time for self-care is hard, but so is suffering from stress and worry. The mountain we choose to climb will be challenging, and there will be moments when we struggle to find the next foothold. But, in the end, we choose what kind of hard we want to live with.

In addition to the latest in psychology and neuroscience, I've packed this book with insights I've gleaned from my conversations with extraordinary achievers. We can learn a great deal from industry titans by examining the trail of choices they left behind. As such, the pages of this book include lessons learned from my conversations with

- Richard Branson, founder of the Virgin Group.

CHOOSING GREATNESS

- Jonathan Johnson, chief executive officer at Overstock.com.

- Lara Merriken, entrepreneur and founder of LÄRABAR.

- Daniel Nestor, winner of eight Grand Slams and an Olympic gold medal in doubles tennis.

- Teena Piccione, global transformation and operations executive at Google.

- Kim Rivera, chief legal officer at OneTrust.

- Javier Rodriguez, chief executive officer at DaVita Inc.

- Eric Severson, chief people and belonging officer at Neiman Marcus Group.

- Everett Thomas, executive at Lockheed Martin, a major general (US Air Force, retired), who survived the Pentagon's bombing during 9/11 and was awarded two medals for supporting the war on terror.

- Phyllis Yale, advisory partner for Bain & Company.

AN INVITATION

Here's the thing: you work hard every day to create the life you've always dreamed of. Leveraging the power of choice will dramatically accelerate your brain's ability to operate at peak efficiency and precision.

Choosing growth changes, well, *everything*.

And that choice, it turns out, is yours.

PART 1

CHOOSING YOUR FUTURE

Author Christina Curtis.

Chapter 1

HAVE YOU BEEN HIJACKED?

Define success on your own terms, achieve it by your own rules, and build a life you're proud to live.

—Anne Sweeney, former President
of the Disney-ABC Television Group

ON A COOL FALL DAY in 2016, I was driving my two young kids to school a little late, having fallen behind after the chaos of the morning. While thinking about the workday ahead, I half-listened to them in the backseat having one of those countless petty arguments as siblings often do. This one was about whom our dog, Becca, liked best.

We stopped at the red light, waiting to turn into the school parking lot, when suddenly, the passenger door flew open and a man with a knife jumped in. As I tried to process what was happening, the twelve-inch blade came at my throat and I screamed, grabbing his arm and his body, pushing both him and the knife away.

He yelled at me to drive, and I quickly obeyed, putting one hand on the wheel, and keeping the other on his wrist. My maternal instincts took over. Protecting my kids was my only priority.

If I get into an accident, people will come, I thought. *Someone will help. Someone will save us.* I hit the gas hard and drove fast toward a pole.

The man used his free hand to take control of the wheel and steer us back onto the road. Running on adrenaline, I swerved again. The more I fought, the more infuriated he became, the blade thrashing precariously between us.

My eleven-year-old son's voice broke through from the back seat.

"Mom, what should I do?" It was almost a whisper, but it shook me to my core. I looked in the rearview mirror. He was frozen, tears streaming down his face.

"Mom?" he asked again. Then I glanced at his nine-year-old sister, her eyes wide open, staring at me with ferocious intensity. She silently mouthed the words I'd said to her so many times over the years: "*You've got this.*" She was pleading for me to fix it, pleading with me to make this right.

In that instant, time stood still. Seeing their little faces snapped me out of my panicked state, and I felt an intense sense of calm wash over me. I took a few deep breaths, relaxed my shoulders, and brought the car to a slow crawl. Then I ran through my choices. With absolute clarity, I knew what I needed to do next: I had to get the kids out of the car.

"Sir, you can do whatever you want. Take me wherever you want to go. But my kids are getting out. I am going to pull over up here at the library." My assertive tone made it clear that this was nonnegotiable. He said no with equal conviction, and I realized the complication. We were in a two-door vehicle. For them to escape to safety, one of us in the front seats would have to exit first. There was no way in hell I would volunteer to leave, and he clearly felt the same way.

He demanded that I turn down the next street, which I knew was tucked away and quiet. In my mind, these instructions spelled disaster. Parking my car where no one else was around felt like too dangerous an approach. But what were my alternatives? Then and there, I decided that my only option was to fight him. If he and I were locked in battle, I could yell at the kids to climb out the windows and run.

But I didn't want my children to see this. I didn't want them to have this memory. As I have consistently done throughout their lives, whether dealing with a tantrum, getting their annual shots, or managing through a bored state of mind, I knew we needed a distraction! I asked the man to grab my phone in the center console so I could dial up a cartoon.

"Kids, want to watch a show? *Kung Fu Panda? Wild Kratts? SpongeBob SquarePants?* What sounds best?" I asked, speaking in a normal, conversational tone.

Our assailant seemed shocked by the request and fidgeted in his seat, his left leg starting to shake nervously. As I continued to force a casual dialogue with my kids, his anxiousness escalated. Perhaps the extent of what he had done was finally starting to sink in. After all, when jumping in the car, given the tinted windows, he would have seen only a female, not a mother and her two children. The seconds slowly ticked away, then out of nowhere, he shouted, "Pull the hell over!"

I veered to the sidewalk, and before the car even came to a stop, he opened the door and ran. I reached over, slammed his car door, and sped off to a friend's house who lived nearby. We went into the house for safety. Everyone was OK. Everyone was all right. Having some trouble breathing, I walked back outside to get some fresh air. The panic had returned with vengeance, and my legs gave out beneath me. I crumpled to the ground and sobbed.

This miserable event left a significant impact on our whole family. Afraid to be alone, we all moved through the house as a pack, even when brushing our teeth. My daughter didn't speak for three days, and my son jumped at any sudden sound or motion. But with time, the incident no longer invaded our every thought, and the edges of the picture began to fray. Perhaps my daughter described it best with the surprising profundity children often muster: the man's face began to melt from our minds like a snowman by the fire.

I grappled with the enormity of what we had

experienced, the reality that my children could have lost their mother that day, or worse, I could have lost them. This realization etched significant changes in the way I approach my life. It kicked the door wide open to the fact that our time is measured in minutes—that an unexpected, life-changing event can overtake the best-made plans. It tapped a deep reservoir of courage and aroused an even deeper commitment to stop watching the days, weeks, and months fall off the calendar.

I share this story with you because it clarified an insight that has shifted the way I see the world and has become foundational to my life's work.

In the middle of our nightmarish encounter, my children interrupted my initial reaction, bringing my conscious mind back into the driver's seat. It wasn't until then that I could see the different options available to me. While luck unquestionably played its part, the neuroscience and psychology I had been studying for years suddenly hit home in a visceral way. The difference between reacting and responding, between reflex and reflection, between habitual response and conscious thought, crystalized.

HAVE YOU BEEN HIJACKED?

In the split second between an event and our reaction to it, is a space that we need to inhabit. That we need to expand. Taking the time to pause and choose the thought or action that will move us toward the greatest outcome. Otherwise, these habits can hijack our decisions without our even realizing it. We end up

Habits can hijack our decisions without our even realizing it.

repeating previously learned behaviors, reentering the coordinates of where we've been versus where we want to go next. It's estimated that roughly 40 percent of our actions each day are driven by habits.[1] The busier and more stressful our lives become, the more we rely on habitual responses that come barreling down our well-honed neural pathways.

These habits lie deep within the brain structure, firing automatically, regardless of whether we want them to or

1 Society for Personality and Social Psychology. "How we form habits, change existing ones." ScienceDaily. (August 8, 2014), www.sciencedaily.com/releases /2014/08/140808111931.htm.

not. Sometimes these pesky patterns may, at first glance, appear trivial—such as looking at your phone, skipping a workout, not preparing, procrastinating, or eating poorly. But when we look at them in various contexts, we can see their true significance—glancing at your phone *while driving*, increasing the likelihood of an accident; skipping a workout *when stressed*, making you more punchy and less productive; procrastinating *on strengthening your relationships*, limiting your level of influence; not *preparing in advance of meetings*, decreasing your overall effectiveness. Heck, one study even found that after a heart attack, only 4.3 percent of participants made all three lifestyle changes recommended by physicians (quitting smoking, eating a healthy diet, and exercising).[2] Despite life-threatening consequences, habitual responses fire on.

Achieving exceptional outcomes in life requires consciously choosing the action or thought that will drive the greatest impact for every minute you spend and ounce of energy you're investing. Discomfort be damned.

Choose.

---

2 Koon Teo et al., (2013). Prevalence of a healthy lifestyle among individuals with cardiovascular disease in high, middle- and low-income countries. *Journal of the American Medical Association* 309(15), April 17, 2013, 1613–1621.

HAVE YOU BEEN HIJACKED?

And if it doesn't go as planned, choose again. No guilt or shame or regret required as you iteratively move your way through growth.

Fortunately, science has shown us the tools we need

Achieving exceptional outcomes in life requires consciously choosing the action or thought that will drive the greatest impact for every minute you spend and ounce of energy you're investing.

to do things differently and the choices required to break through one layer of limitation to the next, then the next, then the next. After all, there's no need to grin and bear it by saying, "I'm fine," in areas where you feel anything *but*. Life's too short, and you work too hard for *fine* to be the future.

As my daughter said, *"You've got this."*

Now, let's get started.

DEEPENING THE WORK

KEY TAKEAWAYS

- The brain creates habits that enable us to perform certain tasks on autopilot, saving our limited neurological fuel.

- Peak performers choose the behaviors required to drive the highest return tomorrow, leaning into the discomfort that comes from choosing change. They choose what kind of hard they want to experience.

- Life is too short to tolerate "fine" when you feel anything but. Avoid the temptation to tolerate mediocrity.

EXPLORATORY QUESTIONS

Take thirty minutes to reflect on what you want to be able to say at the end of your career.

- What accomplishments did you achieve?

- How did you show up?

- What relationships did you build?

- What impact did you have on others?

- How much money did you generate?

- What did your personal life look like?

- How did you integrate career and personal living to maximize your sense of connection, meaning, and fulfillment?

- What is this current phase of your career all about?

TASKS

1. Look for any unproductive automatic behaviors that are occurring without much conscious thought. For example, glancing at your phone when driving or sitting in a meeting.

2. Take a few deep breaths to bring yourself back into the present in order to choose a different behavior. For example, do not look at your phone or even turn the phone off.

3. Observe the thoughts and sensations that immediately follow.

4. Continue to bring awareness to what it feels like when you choose to interrupt a habitual response, getting acquainted with that discomfort and not letting it drive your behaviors.

Richard Branson, founder of the Virgin Group.

Chapter 2

A MEETING WITH THE FUTURE YOU

I learned to always take on things I'd never done before.
Growth and comfort do not coexist.
—GINNI ROMETTY, FORMER CEO OF IBM

....

MY FIRST ENCOUNTER with Richard Branson was at a conference in Denver on the business of empathy. After asking for tips on how to stay fit, the interviewer jokingly challenged Richard to a plank competition. Richard not only accepted the challenge, but at sixty-nine years old, he won, laughing his way through it. *Typical Richard fashion*, I thought. Bold, endearing, and a little bit wild. The audience was immediately hooked.

Through his early struggles with dyslexia, Richard had learned the importance of surrounding himself with talented people, delegating tasks, and consistently taking on bold goals. I wondered if perhaps that sense of feeling behind had helped Richard get ahead, giving him a perspective that others were missing. His stories were imbued with a strong sense of perseverance and a clear thirst for life.

After the interview wrapped up, the audience rose to their feet in a standing ovation. Clearly, Richard had struck a chord. His appeal? Achieving extraordinary levels of success while having a heck of a good time doing it. I knew right then and there that he was a leader I needed to reach out to. And so I did.

When we sat down together, Richard was enjoying some much-needed downtime with his family at his private island. He showed up in a relaxed, white, button-down shirt, taking a seat on the couch as the sun streamed in through the windows. Before the conversation started, he made a point of thanking *me* for taking my time to meet him. *Authentic and approachable*, I noted, scribbling down my observations as I worked to figure out his secret to success.

I asked Richard the most important lesson he had learned over his five decades of being an entrepreneur. He took me back to the summer of 1969, when he was eighteen years old, looking up at the moon. Buzz Aldrin and Neil Armstrong were making their initial descent in the lunar module *Eagle*, becoming the first people to walk on the moon's surface. "That was it," shared Richard. "That was the moment I realized that I wanted to go up there. I am a strong believer in setting those types of bold goals. Without that clarity, I think you just end up achieving less in life."

Over the decades, Richard filled many a notebook with goals that were often born out of frustration—things

....

**"I am a strong believer in setting
those types of bold goals.
Without that clarity,
I think you just end up
achieving less in life."**

....

he wanted to address, to solve, to experience. These goals helped shape the path (or, in his case, the flight plan) to get to where he wanted to go.

We all need goals, though they may not involve strapping oneself into a suborbital spacecraft. Goals infuse our day-to-day activities, guiding our efforts, multiplying the impact of our actions by giving them direction so we don't just move but move forward. They end up being the essential plot points in the stories of our lives, influencing our behaviors and quietly shaping our future.

That's why it's so important to get unapologetically clear on what you want to achieve, sharpening your pencil to write a clear picture of what meeting the "future you" would be like. In the future, what type of work would you be doing? What would your personal life include? How would it feel for others to be around you? What amount of time, money, and joy would you have access to?

By hitting pause long enough to think about the future, you can start setting goals that line up with where you want to go. Perhaps you hope your future self will be running her own company, sitting on boards, or traveling for two months of the year. Or maybe you envision him writing books and working part-time, having already made his millions.

Whatever your vision of your future self may be, these thoughts and dreams will consciously and unconsciously inform your present. That's where goals come in. What goals do you need in place to ultimately move you toward that direction? What skills do you need to sharpen? What brand do you need to build? What energy do you need to exude? What network do you need to be strengthening? What growth do you now need to choose?

To help us get this right, I reached out to Dr. David Rock, cofounder and CEO of the NeuroLeadership Institute. David's research on understanding the brain at

A goal is only useful if it is truly embedded in your thinking.

work has helped move scientific findings into the mainstream, transforming theory into application. "A goal is only useful if it is truly embedded in your thinking," he shared as we spoke. "Only then can it direct your attention and orient the brain toward certain opportunities. Even when you aren't consciously aware of it. Goals prime the brain, making it more aware of relevant information. Things we might not have noticed start popping up around us, serving up opportunities to get there."

Let's say, for example, your goal is to get 25 percent

fitter this year. You might suddenly pay more attention to the set of stairs in your building or notice your colleagues talking about exercise. Maybe you start seeing more gyms or begin looking at different types of running shoes. By clearly defining events that haven't yet happened, you are training your brain to bring about the success you seek.

CRAFTING GOALS WITH PASSION AND PRECISION

Clear goals also take advantage of a glitch in our neurological wiring: the brain's inability to clearly distinguish between what's real and what's imagined. Think about it. The very thought of public speaking can cause our hearts to pound and our throats to tighten, even when there isn't a podium in sight.

Brain scans reveal that images of the future and memories of the past are both generated by the same neural circuitry.[1] Defining that vision of what you want to achieve is like making memories of events that haven't happened yet. They become more realistic, more

---

1 Daniel L. Schacter et al., "The Future of Memory: Remembering, Imagining, and the Brain," *Neuron* 76, no. 4 (November 21, 2012), https://www.ncbi.nlm.nih.gov /pmc/articles/PMC3815616/.

magnetic, even probable, by focusing our attention and efforts toward that future.

Take, for example, my client Jim, a vice president at a manufacturing company. Jim had been running too hard for too long on the achievement treadmill. "I tell my team that it's a marathon, not a sprint . . . but now it feels like we're just sprinting a marathon," he said. "I'm running from meeting to meeting, perpetually putting out fires. Frankly, I'm exhausted."

....

Clear goals also take advantage of a glitch in our neurological wiring: the brain's inability to clearly distinguish between what's real and what's imagined.

....

Jim called me to learn more about executive coaching and whether the process could help him break free of the torrential cycle of nonstop tasks. When I walked into his office, the first thing I noticed was his family—his desk and walls were decorated with photographs of vacations, barbecues, and his daughter's soccer games. This photo collection told the story of a man who had it all, but he didn't look to be enjoying the life he was living. I could see that the edges of his world were beginning to fray.

"I love working hard, but I'm no longer excited," he shared. "No matter what I do, my efforts aren't being noticed. I'm reaching a point of wanting to just throw in the towel. Maybe I'm already there."

Jim had lost touch with where he was headed and why. It was clear that his herculean efforts lacked purpose and precision.

"Jim," I said, breaking the silence. "I see your daughter plays soccer."

He looked surprised by the question. "Yes, she does."

"What's her name?"

"Julia. She's just finishing up her freshman year."

"Let's imagine this," I said. "Julia's out on the field playing the biggest game of her life, but she keeps getting distracted. The coach is yelling. The turf is slick. The other team is trash-talking." I paused. "If you had a chance to pull her aside and give her some guidance, what would you say?"

While I was interested in Jim's family, the true purpose of the question was to interrupt his thinking pattern that was clearly stuck in a negative loop. After a minute of silence, I knew it had worked.

"I would tell her to forget about everything and just focus on the goal at the end of the field," he said.

"OK, let's start there," I stated. "You have a choice to make, Jim. What do you want to be running toward? What's the goal at the end of *your* field?"

And now I direct the same question to you: Where are you headed, and what are *you* running toward?

A SEVEN-POINT SELF-ASSESSMENT

To arrive at your next destination, you need to first identify your current location. This begins by objectively and honestly assessing how the various areas of your work life are going. Taking a quick snapshot helps you see where frustrations are surfacing and what's causing unnecessary friction and slowing you down.

For the following seven categories, rate yourself on a scale of 1 to 10 with 10 being "I'm so satisfied with this area that I'm dancing on a cloud" and 1 being "I think I just threw up a little." What does a snapshot of your current work life look like?

CHOOSING GREATNESS

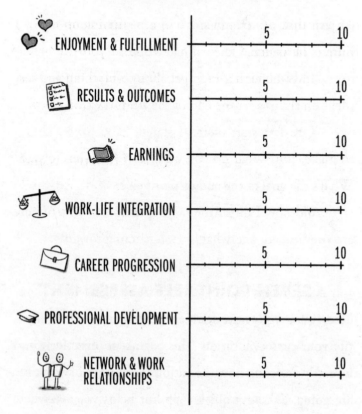

Next, choose one or two areas where you are ready to drive change. Look for those places and spaces where you are tolerating mediocrity, unhappy with the current state.

Take some time to reflect deeply on what the ideal outcome would be. Perhaps you already know the answer; it's been popping into your mind for some time now, like that tune on the radio that's been running on repeat. Muster the courage to jot it down. Turn your thoughts from mind to matter, putting them into black-and-white text. Researchers have shown that simply writing down

....

Goals need to harness and sustain their own motivational energy to overcome the daunting distance between here and there.

....

your goals makes you 42 percent more likely to achieve them.[2] "I'm a great, great believer in writing goals down," Richard Branson explained. "I go back to my old note-books, and there are pages and pages of things I set out to do. When it's on paper, you can use it to plan your day, your week, your month, your year, or even your decade. Write it down, then set out to do it."

Historically, this is where our process of developing goals has fallen short. We make them too clinical and too

---

2 Gail Matthews, "The Impact of Commitment, Accountability, and Written Goals on Goal Achievement," *Dominican Scholar*, Dominican University of California, 2007, https://scholar.dominican.edu/cgi/viewcontent.cgi?article=1002&context =psychology-faculty-conference-presentations.

complicated, failing to consider some fundamental aspects of human nature, such as motivation and memory.

Goals need to harness and sustain their own motivational energy to overcome the daunting distance between here and there. "If you don't have passion for it, it's not the right thing to go after," shared Richard. After all, human beings are not robots who will do something just because they are told—even if we are the ones giving the orders!

Frame goals not just in terms of what needs to be achieved, but why. This primes the brain to focus on the impact those goals are driving, activating the effort and energy you need to achieve them. To further embed these goals into your psyche, also be sure to make them easy to recite and remember, whittling down the words like a ruthless editor. How would you describe what you want to achieve in thirty words or fewer?

"The biggest impact of a goal is its influence on the unconscious," Dr. David Rock explained. "That only happens when the goal is super easy to remember and emotionally enticing so that it's consistently influencing our behaviors behind the scenes."

A MEETING WITH THE FUTURE YOU

Here are three other tactics to make the process as effective as possible:

Add a noun to the key words instead of just a verb. For example, researchers were able to increase voter turnout at statewide elections by phrasing the questions around "being a voter" versus "voting."[3] Let's use this to our advantage, weaving in our identity to enhance our probability of success.

Use active language that is present based, replacing phrases such as *I'll try* or *I will* with *I am*. This signals to the brain that the goal is currently in process. One study found those who believed they had already made progress were twice as likely to achieve their goal as those who thought they were starting from scratch.[4] The feeling of being one step closer to the finish line can jump-start your motivational engine and keep you flying forward

---

3   C. J. Bryan, G. M. Walton, T. Rogers, and C. S. Dweck, "Motivating Voter Turnout by Invoking the Self," *Proceedings of the National Academy of Sciences* 108, no. 31 (2011): 12653–56.

4   Ran Kivetz, Oleg Urminsky, and Yuhuang Zheng, "The Goal-Gradient Hypothesis Resurrected: Purchase Acceleration, Illusionary Goal Progress, and Customer Retention," *Journal of Marketing Research* 43 (February 2006): 39–58, http://home .uchicago.edu/ourminsky/Goal-Gradient_Illusionary_Goal_Progress.pdf.

Be careful not to write your goals in terms of what you want to avoid. Examples? Not wanting to be stressed out all the time, not wanting to spend too much money, and not wanting to feel out of shape. Avoidance goals lead to increased procrastination and less likelihood of success[5]—there simply isn't as clear a path from avoidance to achievement. Imagine you were climbing a mountain. If your only goal was not to fall off the side of the mountain, how likely would you be to reach the summit?

Once you have written down your simple statement, tape it to your computer, drop it into your wallet,

....

If your only goal was not to fall off the side of the mountain, how likely would you be to reach the summit?

....

and put it on your closet door. Make sure it's visible so the words seep into your thinking and prime your brain

5 Martin Oscarsson, Per Carlbring, Gerhard Andersson, and Alexander Rozental, "A Large-Scale Experiment on New Year's Resolutions: Approach-Oriented Goals Are More Successful Than Avoidance-Oriented Goals," *PLoS One* 15, no. 12 (2020), https://www.ncbi.nlm.nih.gov/pmc/articles/PMC7725288/.

on what to see and do each day. These few words are part of *you* now.

Jim, my client, had been hyperfocused on what he didn't want and hadn't spent time framing out what he was running toward. Eventually we uncovered that he really wanted to get promoted, be in excellent shape, and increase the amount of quality time he spends with his family. During our next meeting, he thought about how to articulate those aspirations into goals written with passion and precision. By the time he walked me to the elevator, his shoulders had relaxed, and his head was held high. "Focus on the goal at the end of the field," he said. Then the elevator doors closed.

Having clear goals pushed Jim to let go of low-priority tasks and build a more focused portfolio at work for himself and his team. He prioritized daily exercise and held one-on-one meetings while walking to burn off excess stress. He became more engaged at home by increasing the quality of time with family by asking more questions and taking each person out individually once a month to really check in.

By the end of the year, he not only felt happier but

also had been promoted. Jim had chosen to refocus his energy on the end of the field—and he scored.

Choosing what you want to achieve in your career helps you transform that mishmash of snapshots, of *maybes*, of hopeful ambitions from grayscale into popping Technicolor. The result is a vision so sharp and bright that you begin to see not only the summit but also the footholds required to get there.

....

Transform that mishmash of snapshots, of maybes, of hopeful ambitions from grayscale into popping Technicolor.

....

In the summer of 1969, a teenage Richard Branson gazed up at the moon, imagining the Apollo astronauts exploring its surface, and hatched the beginnings of a plan to one day venture into space. Fifty-one years later, he was floating weightless fifty-three miles above the earth, having kicked open the door to a brand-new astrotourism industry. One small step for Richard, one giant leap for mankind, one might say.

How high do you want your orbit?

Think big. Be bold. Choose goals worthy of you, goals that inspire every cell of your body to fly forward with passion and precision. Write them down and treat them with reverence, using their force to propel you at an awe-inspiring pace toward that meeting with the future you.

DEEPENING THE WORK

....

KEY TAKEAWAYS

- Get clear on what you want your future to look like.

- Write that vision down into goal statements infused with passion and precision.

- Keep goals simple so they become embedded in your thinking and serve to orient you toward opportunities you might otherwise have missed.

- Avoid goals that refer to what you *don't* want. There is no clear path from avoidance to achievement.

- Replace weasel words such as *I'll try* with *I am* so your brain understands you're already on the road to get there.

- Put your goals somewhere visible so when the going gets rough, your North Star will still be bright enough to guide you forward.

EXPLORATORY QUESTIONS

1. What two or three things do you want to accomplish in the next twelve months so that you feel like it was a successful year?

2. How are these accomplishments aligned with who you are as a person and the life you want to be living?

3. How can you write these desired accomplishments in the form of a goal that is both memorable and motivating?

4. What are the individual phases of each goal? Break them down into a minimum of four to six milestones.

TASKS

- Take ten days to reflect on these answers further, giving yourself the time and space to process at a deeper level.

- Tell someone you trust about the goals. Let them know you are looking for an advocate, supporter, and thought partner.

- Put the goal statements somewhere you can see them every day.

- Expect setbacks! These are part of the process. Look for what you can learn and move through these moments with compassion. More to come on this in the chapters to follow!

PART 2

CHOOSING YOUR FOCUS

Javier Rodriguez, chief executive officer of DaVita Inc.

Chapter 3

SHARP FOCUS, BRIGHT FUTURE

I wake up every morning and think to myself,
"How far can I push the company forward
in the next twenty-four hours?"
—*Leah Busque, founder of TaskRabbit*

EVER HAD ONE of those days (or decades) where you were constantly working but not getting enough done? You're not alone. Many of us wake up to a full inbox before we've even had our morning coffee, with the day quickly becoming a dumping ground for chores, tasks, and meetings. We continue to play Whac-A-Mole with calendar invites, text messages, and emails streaming in, only to be distracted by the never-ending barrage of things to do—the tyranny of the urgent—as we move from one thing to the next.

CHOOSING GREATNESS

But there is no prize for the most volume managed. One can't reach exceptional heights while being weighed down by this kind of *busy*. After all, the brain only has so much cognitive bandwidth available to invest before our intelligence dims and our decision-making suffers—we become more reactive, impulsive, and automatic in our

....

There is no prize for the most volume managed.

....

approach.[1] How can we protect our energy and time to consistently put our best thinking forward?

To explore this further, I reached out to Javier Rodriguez. Javier is the CEO of DaVita, a kidney care company with over 62,000 teammates across twelve countries. It's hard to imagine having such a sizable job and the responsibilities that come with it; there is no shortage of things to get done.

---

1 Vicki R. LeBlanc, "The Effects of Acute Stress on Performance: Implications for Health Professions Education," *Academic Medicine* 84, no. 10 (October 2009): S25–S33, https://journals.lww.com/academicmedicine/fulltext/2009/10001/the _effects_of_acute_stress_on_performance_.8.aspx.

SHARP FOCUS, BRIGHT FUTURE

Yet despite all the pressures of being a CEO, Javier shows up year after year as a leader I would be honored to follow. He is thoughtful, inspiring, and in service of others, consistently coming to meetings both present and prepared. I often wonder if he has somehow managed to develop a different relationship with time.

"We have an opportunity in front of us to do something really meaningful in life," Javier shared as we spoke. "And we'll never know how much time we have to do it. So I wake up energized every day to do great things with others, using my time in a way that allows me to make the best of it."

As the CEO of a company that's dedicated to improving patients' lives, Javier can't afford to be *somewhat* efficient and effective; there's just too much at stake. How does he manage the demands of his day?

"The key is to develop an instinct around value," he shared. "I give myself permission to ask meaningful questions on what will drive the greatest impact for the teammates and patients we serve. Then I rearrange the week based on the answers, keeping my eye on those goals so I don't get distracted."

Javier moved to the United States from Mexico in

seventh grade and had to adjust to the new norms and rebuild his community. With a passion for purpose, he followed his dad's advice to consistently think like an owner, regardless of the job he was in. It wasn't about being a manager, director, vice president, or CEO but about looking for ways to make a meaningful difference.

"We all have dreams of our lives mattering," Javier explained. "Of having a bigger purpose. Once you know what your purpose is, figure out where you can fulfill it. Wherever the biggest challenge is, that's where you need to go. Run to that fire."

Javier sharpens his focus externally with an eye toward value and impact and internally by choosing the right level of energy to bring to each engagement.

"Energy is the most contagious thing in life, regardless of whether it's up or down," he shared. "I hold myself accountable for the energy I bring into every conversation. At the end of the day, I ask myself, *Was I a producer of positive energy today? Or did I consume the energy of others?* We can't look to those around us to drive the excitement. We need to be the one that walks in energized, ready to tackle whatever challenge presents itself."

SHARP FOCUS, BRIGHT FUTURE

When it comes to achieving exceptional results, energy is essential. After all, being talented is only meaningful when someone is motivated to apply that talent to a problem. Research has shown that energizing emotions act like electricity running through the neurological wires of the group, maximizing individual and group performances[2]—sparking ideation, excitement, and drive. As Javier shared, these emotions are contagious. In fact, a twenty-year longitudinal study was able to clearly identify groups of happiness and unhappiness across a community, with negative people being surrounded by clusters of negativity and positive people being surrounded by clusters of positivity.[3] To maximize performance and outcomes, we need to consciously enhance the emotional landscape around us. The best emotion to bring depends on the primary objective of the engagement, whether it's

---

2 See Peter Schulman, "Applying Learned Optimism to Increase Sales Productivity," *Journal of Personal Selling and Sales Management* 19, no. 1 (Winter 1999): 31–37, https://www.jstor.org/stable/40471704; M. E.; A. M. Isen, "Positive Affect," in *Handbook of Cognition and Emotion*, eds. T. Dalgleish and M. J. Power (New York: John Wiley & Sons, 1999), 521–539, https://doi.org/10.1002/0470013494.ch25; and Qishan Chen et al., "How Leaders' Psychological Capital Influence Their Followers' Psychological Capital: Social Exchange or Emotional Contagion," *Frontiers in Psychology*, July 12, 2019, https://www.frontiersin.org/articles/10.3389/fpsyg.2019.01578/full.

3 "Framingham Heart Study (FHS)," National Heart, Lung, and Blood Institute, https://www.nhlbi.nih.gov/science/framingham-heart-study-fhs.

brainstorming, innovation, execution, or analysis. Choose the energy that will enable the room to untangle the problem it's facing by projecting your own sense of excitement, joy, connectedness, curiosity, gratitude, or hope.

You see, driving exceptional outcomes isn't about going faster or doing more; it requires focused intensity. Rather than scattering your energy and efforts across too many priorities, choose which ones will drive the greatest impact in relation to your goals, and channel all your effort and intellect there. Just think of the sun. It

Sharpen your focus through the lens of value and light your own goals on fire.

doesn't burn the leaves on the ground until you hold a magnifying glass at just the right angle. The glass then concentrates the heat, and within seconds, you have a flame. Let us not say yes to too many things, taking on everything and diffusing our effectiveness. Instead, sharpen your focus through the lens of value, and light your own goals on fire.

SHARP FOCUS, BRIGHT FUTURE

PRIORITIZING VALUE OVER VOLUME

Scientists and management gurus alike understand the negative impacts of taking on too much. The volume can feel overwhelming as we run from one thing to the next, leading to less adaptive and more reactive behaviors, not to mention substandard execution and feelings of discouragement.[4] *How can I be working so hard and still not be getting ahead of it all?* The drudgery of ill-performing projects can even push us to start new ones, seeking the excitement from the shiny new toy.

Continuously draining our most critical resource, the brain, doesn't honor the unbendable rules of human biology.

A simple phrase to remember throughout your day is *value over volume*.

As we will explore in chapter 4, the brain has a limited amount of working memory to invest in any twenty-four-hour period. By being too busy, we deplete ourselves of the

4 Steyn, H. and Schnetler, Rohann, "Concurrent projects: How many can you handle?" *The South African Journal of Industrial Engineering*. 26. 10.7166/26-3-1104, (2015). https://www.researchgate.net/publication/285549936_Concurrent_projects_How_many_can_you_handle/link/566bf95c08ae1a797e3d25b8/download.

neurological resources required to drive exceptional insights and outcomes. Neuroscientists call it cognitive overload. We can call it IQ-siphoning, intelligence-sabotaging, or dumbing ourselves down. Whatever label we use, we end up treating our brain like a beat-up car and those around us more like pylons than people, losing our ability to apply our strongest thinking to the most important problems.

A simple phrase to remember throughout your day is *value over volume*. Where will you get the greatest return on your effort, energy, and intellect today? Start with your goals in mind and the type of value you are seeking to generate, using that as a lens to see which activities will have the greatest likelihood of getting you to where you want to go.

This concept came to mind after a conversation I had with Lara Merriken, an inspiring entrepreneur who created the national bestselling snack LÄRABAR. As we sat on a patio enjoying a glass of wine, she walked me back to when her business first started.

Lara was hiking in the Colorado mountains eating a package of trail mix and feeling less than enthused by the flavors and ingredients. She had been wrestling with what to do in life, looking to shift toward a career that could have an even greater impact on doing good in the world. As a health enthusiast, she asked herself, *What if I could create a healthy snack that people were excited to snack on?* She ran home, jotted down ideas, and started playing with the concept of combining fruit, nuts, and spices into a tasty treat.

Lara Merriken, founder of LÄRABAR.

Lara invested her time in the activities that would drive the highest value for her business. She spent hours playing with different combinations of ingredients. She engaged friends and family in focus groups to see which flavors they liked best and why. She wrote ideas in her journal, strategizing on how to talk about the snack bar in a way that would generate excitement. She even quit her job to start working the floor at Whole Foods. "At the time, I knew nothing about the food industry. I had to put myself in the best place where I could learn," she shared.

CHOOSING GREATNESS

Lara's focused intensity paid off. During an early morning shift, she was taking out the recycling boxes when a key buyer walked in. Having met before, they exchanged pleasantries.

"I remember thinking, *This is it, Lara. This is your shot*," she shared. Lara began telling the buyer about her snack bar and noticed him initially backing away. Clearly, he hadn't expected anything more than friendly banter. But Lara pushed on, and he ended up asking for a sample. The buyer's reaction? It was one of the most innovative products he'd tried in years. "Here's my card," he said. "When you're ready, give me a call."

Lara used her goal—creating a tasty, healthful, indulgent snack bar—as a guide to find the highest-value activities, prioritizing her time accordingly. Two years later, LÄRABAR filled the shelves of supermarkets across the country, and sales reached $7.1 million. A year after that, she sold the company to General Mills.

"Some days it was hard to figure out where to focus when everything felt like a fire," Lara shared. "Then I started to recognize what a real fire was—and wasn't. What moved the business forward and what didn't. Not getting a shipment to a major retailer? That's a 911—drop everything to solve it. But a lot of other things can wait, and some things don't need to be done at all."

To identify where the value lies in your world, start by going back to the goals you defined in the previous chapter. Before we go any further, let's quickly cover some terminology:

- **Goal:** The desired outcome you want to achieve.

- **High-impact initiatives:** Each of your goals will have three to five of these high-impact initiatives that move the goal forward. They are the vehicles for all your activities and are time-bound and measurable.

- **Activities:** The list of activities that make up your high-impact initiatives.

Here is an example:

- **Goal:** Get promoted next year.

- **High-impact initiative:** Driving a project that delivers meaningful business value.

- **Activities:** Set meetings with various stakeholders to better understand the strategic focus of the company, speak with your boss to explore what projects you can work on, define what success of that project could look like, engage others for help on getting things done.

In Lara's case, it would have looked something like this:

- **Goal:** Create a highly profitable snack bar company with bars that are tasty and nutritious.

- **High-impact initiatives:** (1) Create the best healthy snack bar recipe in the world, and (2) Drive x number of sales by y date.

- **Activities:** Host focus groups, try different recipes, work at Whole Foods to learn the industry, network with potential buyers, craft a value proposition that entices people to buy in.

Without clarity on the most important things, you walk headfirst into a classic logjam, blocking the path to true success. When we say yes to too much, our goals aren't the only things that suffer. We lose time for ourselves, our families, our friends, our health, and our overall ability to be in the moment. If something doesn't align with our priorities, it has to go, and it's nothing personal.

SHARP FOCUS, BRIGHT FUTURE

....

**Without clarity on the most
important things, you walk
headfirst into a classic logjam,
blocking the path to true success.**

....

"I am still someone who will frequently ask myself, *Why am I doing this?*" shared Lara. "By constantly questioning, evaluating, and analyzing, I don't end up putting my energy into things that aren't important. There's just no time for that."

PULLING IT ALL TOGETHER: THE WEEKLY CALENDAR AUDIT

A discerning audit of your focus areas is critical. To manage all these elements, use the tool that serves as a blueprint of your life: the calendar. Your calendar is the only place where you can be in the past, present, and future simultaneously to assess and optimize where that value lies.

"The calendar review sounds more administrative than strategic—but it should be done with an eye toward value and impact, not time allocation," shared Javier. "It's about digging in and asking, *Where and how am I generating value?*

Where in the business are disruption or discontinuity needed, and am I investing the right amount of time there? What has to be added, what has to shrink, and what has to go?"

Calendar planning allows you to redraw the map on how you are investing your time until it consistently leads you to treasures. Dedicate a full hour to this task each week to perform some thorough, honest, brutal

....

Calendar planning allows you to redraw the map on how you are investing your time until it consistently leads you to treasures.

....

accounting. This is your chance to look ahead and see if you've created optimal conditions for stellar performance by doing the following:

- **Look at the bigger picture.** Where are you double (or triple) booked? What days are you unable to eat? Where did you forget to include exercise or date nights? When are you so busy you won't be able to get any important work done? The calendar is a visual aid that allows you to easily shift, flip, and delete activities that aren't moving you in the right direction.

- **Meld the personal and professional.** Don't forget to put your personal and professional lives into a single place. This all-in-one approach gets everything out in the open, putting any unproductive habits on full display. For example, if you are dropping off your kids before getting to your first call but haven't scheduled the time it takes to get to work, you are automatically setting yourself up for stress and struggle—until we invent teleporters, like the ones in *Star Trek*. Otherwise, the calendar can end up looking more like an obstacle course than a workweek.

- **Integrate the to-do list.** During each calendar review, bring your to-do list into the process by blocking off time to get those key things done. This ensures the task list doesn't lie dormant on your desk, and it enforces prioritization. When slotting tasks into a work block, you have to look at the entire week and say, "Is this important enough to spend my time on, given everything else I have going on? Does it tie into one of my highest-impact initiatives?"

CHOOSING GREATNESS

"It all comes down to discipline," shared Javier. "I grab at least an hour a week to plan out my calendar, looking through the lens of what we need to achieve and seeing how much time I am spending there. Just last week I reviewed the next three months to see what was or wasn't set up effectively."

When we overstuff our calendars with obligations, we create a dysfunctional relationship with time—stretched thin, working hard, yet still feeling guilty about not giving the right level of attention to the right places. To use your time as effectively as possible, you need to make the calendar the ultimate sidekick—the Robin to your Batman, the Goose to your Maverick, the Garfunkel to your Simon.

The weekly calendar audit is one of the most effective practices in the productivity tool kit, screening out what doesn't need to make the cut. Otherwise, we're like a talented maestro leading an orchestra that hasn't yet studied the music. No matter how hard we try, the melody of the day gets jumbled, the harmonies discordant, and we're left with nothing more than a whole lot of noise. No pauses, no pacing, no point.

"When I get distracted and not focused, I can feel

it," shared Javier. "I am much less effective. And look, at the end of the day, I am just another guy who gets up and works hard. Maybe that's the nugget. You don't have to be super smart to be successful, you just need passion, focus, and a strong commitment to your life."

Bottom line, busy is not a badge of honor or a metric for success. The brain has only a finite amount of working memory between rests to direct toward tasks. Sharpening your focus requires stepping back to ask those meaningful

....

Busy is not a badge of honor or a metric for success.

....

questions about where the value lies, then bringing the energy required to drive your high-impact initiatives forward. These are the foundational stones you need to build the week around, allowing the rest of the tasks to simply flow by. Only then can you avoid getting sucked into the undertow of overengagement when another week's torrent comes rushing in.

DEEPENING THE WORK

....

KEY TAKEAWAYS

- Sharpening your focus means making conscious choices about what high-impact initiatives bring the greatest return in the service of your longer-term goals.

- For the greatest success, align your daily activities with your high-impact initiatives, and your high-impact initiatives with your long-term goals.

- A calendar audit is essential to root out the junk food of your day.

- A calendar audit will enable you to recognize activities you're neglecting, the time you're wasting, and the dead ends you're following.

- The key to this is ensuring that all your activities are captured in one snapshot. This means merging your home and work lives, counter to common wisdom.

- A brutal accounting of your time can quickly and profoundly change your trajectory.

- The overarching principle for focused intensity? *Value over volume.*

EXPLORATORY QUESTIONS

1. It's time to invest more focus, effort, and energy in the areas that generate the most value in relation to our goals. To harken back to the famous Pareto principle, if roughly 20 percent of our effects drive 80 percent of our outcomes, let's figure out what that 20 percent is and double down there!

2. What are the high-impact initiatives that will move you further, faster toward your goals?

3. Take time to brainstorm a list of twenty activities you could do to drive a particular high-impact initiative forward. No judgment or "yeah, but" comments allowed. Instead, let your imagination have some fun with it!

4. Which three activities on that list will be most impactful to your progress, generating the greatest return on effort?

TASKS

1. Put the activities you selected right onto the calendar, mapping out when and where they'll be accomplished.

2. Be sure that they are slotted into a time of day when your thinking is at its best.

3. Now protect that time to get these things done! They are of the utmost importance to your long-term goals!

Eric Severson, chief people and belonging officer
at Neiman Marcus Group.

Chapter 4

MANAGING YOUR ENERGY

I must govern the clock. Not be governed by it.

—*GOLDA MEIR, FOURTH PRIME MINISTER OF ISRAEL*

....

"I SUBSCRIBE to the idea of athleticism of the brain," Eric Severson explained as we sat down to talk about professional growth. "Our real competitive advantage lies in how we manage the mind as a resource."

Eric's evidence-based approaches to enhancing performance have been featured in the *Wall Street Journal*, *Businessweek*, the *New York Times*, and the *Washington Post*, and he is currently the chief people and belonging officer at Neiman Marcus Group.

"I don't accept the notion that to be successful, we have to run ourselves into the ground," explained Eric.

CHOOSING GREATNESS

"Continuously feeling overwhelmed is not a recipe for success or happiness."

Those who achieve exceptional outcomes create the daily conditions required to unlock their highest-quality thinking, leveraging the mind as their greatest resource. It's no different than the way professional athletes create the regimens required to maximize speed, agility, and

....

Those who achieve exceptional outcomes create the daily conditions required to unlock their highest-quality thinking, leveraging the mind as their greatest resource.

....

strength. Why is a daily regime so incredibly important? To answer that, we'll need to start by understanding the science behind the brain.

Much like a muscle, the brain can give only so much before giving out. That's why professional weightlifters aren't doing bicep curls for twelve hours straight. Working out too hard leads to injury and burnout. Working out too lightly results in little to no growth. Athletes stress their muscles just long enough to create microtears that cinch back together even stronger, managing the muscle's time under tension—and the same rules apply to the three pounds of matter we have in our head.

Imagine for a moment that you're a star NFL quarterback surrounded by burly offensive linemen. If the quarterback is your brain, the chaos on the field is your life. Your job is to throw the perfect pass into the end zone, despite the three-hundred-pound warriors charging at you. Before you even step on the field, you need a well-crafted game plan on how to execute. Hail Marys may make for good TV, but they're an unreliable life strategy.

TIME-BLOCKING
YOUR BEST 240 MINUTES

Neuroscientists estimate that the brain can engage in around three to five hours of deep, focused work every day.[1] That equates to around 240 minutes of *High-Octane Thinking (HOT) Spots*, when your brain is revving at a much higher frequency. These HOT Spots can vary day

---

1 Keri Wiginton, "Your Ability to Focus May Be Limited to 4 or 5 Hours a Day. Here's How to Make the Most of Them," *The Washington Post*, June 1, 2021, https://www.washingtonpost.com/lifestyle/wellness/productivity-focus-work -tips/2021/05/31/07453934-bfd0-11eb-b26e-53663e6be6ff_story.html.

to day, sometimes showing up after a good night's sleep, an exciting meeting, or a workout. They are also influenced by the nature of your circadian rhythm, the inner clock that regulates the peaks and valleys of your energy and alertness. Some tend to experience greater clarity in the morning when the world has yet to generate its plethora of distractions. Others find they experience improved focus later in the afternoon when the intensity of the day begins to subside. Understanding your own circadian rhythms is an important step to creating optimal conditions; interestingly, these rhythms are genetically determined and remain fairly consistent over the course of one's lifetime.[2]

Bringing awareness to when these surges of clarity and energy occur will allow you to plan your days accordingly. One of my clients, Thomas, finds 5:30 to 7:30 a.m. to be a HOT Spot, when he is most productive and sharp. His mind is racing with ideas, and his creative juices are flowing. He goes to bed at 9:00 p.m. to make sure he has access to this energy.

Another client, Elise, finds that a HOT Spot ramps

---

2 Melissa Lee Phillips, "Circadian Rhythms: Of Owls, Larks and Alarm Clocks," *Nature* 458 (2009): 142–44, https://www.nature.com/articles/458142a.

up in the evening from 7:00 to 9:00 p.m. So she schedules her day to do afterschool pickup and to spend time with her kids until dinner is done, then she curls up with her laptop to access her most brilliant thinking.

When I connected with Dr. David Rock, he spoke about the importance of knowing and understanding your inner rhythms. "The people who do well pay a lot of attention to their attention," he explained. "For example, I got up this morning with a lot of clarity. That's a signal for me to change my plans and sit down to harness that energy."

Those 240 minutes of high-octane thinking are more precious to us than gold. Build your schedule in a way that gives your highest-priority work VIP access to these times on your calendar, putting aside email or scrolling through social media. Other tasks can only get slotted after the royals have been seated. Then let people know about those little time bunkers so you can protect them from interruptions! You'll be surprised how others will respect it and buy in, perhaps using the concept to protect their own HOT Spot focus areas in the day as well. Be the change you want to see, as the saying goes.

CARVING OUT TIME TO THINK

Reaching extraordinary heights requires a combination of thinking and doing. For many of us, "thinking time" may seem like a luxury we can't afford. Or maybe we believe, *I'm thinking all day, so what are we even talking about here?*

Yet in a survey of five hundred leaders, 96 percent of participants reported they lacked time for strategic thinking.[3] When we have less time to think, we are less likely to learn and more prone to falling into the trap of doing what we've always done. It's important to carve out time for deep thinking and reflection; this allows the brain the space it needs to integrate information and make meaningful connections.

When we have less time to think, we are less likely to learn and more prone to falling into the trap of doing what we've always done.

We all know that satisfying feeling we get when we finally achieve clarity on an issue. That moment when

---

3 Rich Horwath, "The Strategic Thinking Manifesto," Strategic Thinking Institute, https://www.strategyskills.com/pdf/The-Strategic-Thinking-Manifesto.pdf?gclid= -CIaV2fG0v88CFcVlfgodSBUM8A.

connections click and the clouds part, revealing an insight that had been hidden from view. *Aha! I got it! I figured it out!* Interestingly, these moments of insight can be seen on brain scans as bright bursts of activity in the regions responsible for information integration, memory creation, and high-level cognitive processing.[4] They are often accompanied by a surge of excitement as our reward system is activated, giving us a dopamine hit to celebrate our newfound clarity.

To create more of these magical "aha" moments, we can't just sit at a desk and hope for a stroke of brilliance. Rather, science has taught us a few tactics to help create the conditions for ideas to take hold:

- **Frame the problem you are working on as a question.** A question will lodge itself in your brain, waiting to be answered.

- **Take a walk**, which a Stanford study found significantly increases creative thinking.[5] The mind can drift in and out of focusing on the problem, giving the subconscious enough time to connect dots.

4 "New Insights on Insight in the Brain," National Science Foundation, July 3, 2018, https://www.nsf.gov/discoveries/disc_summ.jsp?cntn_id=295911.

5 May Wong, "Stanford Study Finds Walking Improves Creativity," *Stanford News*, April 24, 2014, https://news.stanford.edu/2014/04/24/walking-vs-sitting-042414/.

- **Write your ideas down without judgment**, examining them in a two-dimensional format. Jot down thoughts in a journal or, if you don't have one handy, on the back of a napkin in your favorite coffee shop. Visually looking at your thoughts in 2D can help you see gaps or make further connections.

- **Talk it out** by running a whiteboarding session with a colleague to think out loud and link ideas. Out-loud thinking has been shown to not only deepen understanding but also enhance our overall problem-solving capabilities, even when we are just talking to ourselves.

In today's business environment, thinking power is *the* currency for success. Carve out time in your week to mine your brain as a resource, unlocking the insights that can launch you forward further and faster.

MANAGING THE BLIPS AND BLEEPS

OK, folks, time to get uncomfortable. We need to talk about taming the never-ending deluge of digital information that is constantly puppeteering our attention from one thing to the next. While I am the first to admit that I love my devices, it's important to call out that without boundaries in place, we are constantly besieged by attention-seeking electronics. This drains our neurological reserves even when it isn't our primary focus—such as when we are in a meeting when someone's phone lights up, on a call when a notification goes off, or sitting with someone at a restaurant while a television is streaming in the background.

If we don't acknowledge these unwelcome interruptions, we won't be able to make a dent in managing our

Without boundaries in place, we are constantly besieged by attention-seeking electronics.

neurological resources efficiently. It's almost impossible to focus when we're living in a constant state of distraction and noise, unable to give any one task, problem, or person the attention required.

And look, we come to this discussion from a place of good intent. We don't mean to lose time and damage our relationships and overall effectiveness by using electronics. But have you ever noticed how you meant to spend two minutes checking your email or googling something only to disappear down a rabbit hole for twenty? Or sat down to complete a project when a call comes in, and the next thing you know that focused time is gone—along with any opportunity to do what you had originally intended? Or been in a discussion with someone who keeps glancing at their phone, leading you to feel undervalued or unappreciated?

We live our lives in thrall to distractions—the junk food of our schedules—reaching for our phones ninety-six times a day.[6] That's roughly once every ten minutes! This voluntary and persistent interruption pulls us out of the present and into other tasks and places. This not only is unproductive, but ironically our drive to stay connected also ends up eroding the very relationships we think we're maintaining by staying in touch.

And yet I'll be the first to admit, phone addiction is a hard habit to break. I suffer from it frequently. The hyperarousal we experience can be energizing, even fun. There's a biological reason for this: the positive stimulation we get from these activities generates a release of dopamine that quietly reinforces our addiction, to the point that we can

6 "Americans Check Their Phones 96 Times a Day," Asurion, November 21, 2019, https://www.asurion.com/press-releases/americans-check-their-phones-96-times-a-day/.

feel a sense of dread or panic whenever our device is out of sight.[7]

Eric Severson believes that cutting through the chaos requires choosing a highly disciplined process. "Text messages, phone calls, and the constant noises of notifications have all become so integrated into our lives that we don't even think about the consequences. I intentionally choose what I'm doing and invest my full attention there. If I'm walking the dog, in a meeting, watching TV, or working on a task, I don't use my phone simultaneously."

Eric has learned firsthand that multitasking is an ineffective and costly strategy. Scientists have found that mentally juggling two tasks requires the brain to reset the rules applied to each problem in quick succession, costing us as much as 40 percent of our productivity as the brain switches back and forth.[8]

The solution?

- Choose what you are going to focus on and protect that time.

---

7 Trevor Haynes, "Dopamine, Smartphones & You: A Battle for Your Time," *Science in the News* (blog), May 1, 2018, https://sitn.hms.harvard.edu/flash/2018/dopamine-smartphones-battle-time/.

8 "Multitasking: Switching Costs," American Psychological Association, March 20, 2006, https://www.apa.org/topics/research/multitasking.

- Turn off notifications and let other people know when you are unavailable.

- Proactively decide when in the day to tackle emails, respond to voicemails, or scroll through your social media feeds.

- Turn the phone off periodically and commit to when you will look at it again.

- Admit when you are addicted (raising my hand here) without defending yourself or deflecting blame. Awareness is everything.

- Take technology breaks throughout the month, even if it's for a few hours.

Using these strategies and others to calm the digital buzz will allow you to be more fully engaged in the present and deeply focused, minimizing the likelihood of mistakes, decreasing stress on your system, and keeping you truly connected to yourself and others in real time.

MAKING MEETINGS MEANINGFUL

Another surefire way to lose time and drain thinking power is by going to meetings without much planning or preparation. One survey of managers found that 71 percent of meetings are seen as unproductive.[9] We can no longer blindly move from meeting to meeting without consciously choosing to get more from those minutes!

Here are a few strategies:

- **Set clear objectives.** Send the meeting owner a quick email in advance to request clarity about the meeting's objectives and agenda. This benefits them as well as you because it helps to get everyone aligned and organized. If you're the one who scheduled the meeting, provide that clarity yourself by putting the information right into the invitation.

- **Prepare for all meetings.** Look at your upcoming meetings and write two or three talking points you want to cover in those discussions. You can put these into a notebook or on the calendar alongside the meeting invitation itself.

- **Allocate time effectively.** Ensure that you're allocating the right amount of time to tackle a topic; thirty- and

---

9 Leslie A. Perlow, Constance Noonan Hadley, and Eunice Eun, "Stop the Meeting Madness," *Harvard Business Review*, July–August 2017, https://hbr.org/2017/07/stop -the-meeting-madness.

sixty-minute blocks are not your only options. Maybe all you need is five minutes, or maybe it's twenty-five; whatever the case, it's worth thinking through.

- **Build in breaks.** Leave a five- to ten-minute block between the end of one meeting and the beginning of the next one to allow the brain a moment to reset and regroup.

DO, DELEGATE, DEFER, OR DELETE?

We can't talk about productivity and mastering our minutes without reflecting on what it is we are choosing to take on. One of the hallmark characteristics of a high achiever is the belief that we can do it all ourselves. I get it. You wouldn't have gotten where you are today if you weren't highly capable. But being *able* to do something doesn't necessarily mean you *should* do it—and not every job needs to be done at all.

Richard Branson underlined this important point during our recent conversation. He shared how a young CEO had recently asked him for advice. The CEO was working eighteen hours a day and getting hardly any sleep. Richard recommended that, over the next month, he track the tasks he was working on. "I was willing to bet that at the end of those four weeks, he'd look at those activities and think, *I could have delegated 90 percent of this!* That could free him up to be more creative, spend time with friends and family, and push the business into new areas."

Richard Branson.

We not only need to delegate work that is best done by others but also need to stop accumulating tasks that aren't even ours to begin with. There was a classic 1999 article in *Harvard Business Review* on this very topic called "Management Time: Who's Got the Monkey?" and it goes like this: Someone tells you about a problem they are wrestling with or task they are having a difficult time completing. For one reason or another, you take it over, and in that instant, the problem—or monkey on their back—jumps on to yours.[10]

---

10 William Oncken Jr. and Donald L. Wass, "Management Time: Who's Got the Monkey?," *Harvard Business Review*, November–December 1999, https://hbr.org/1999/11/management-time-whos-got-the-monkey.

CHOOSING GREATNESS

Some people have a real knack for collecting other people's monkeys. If you're one of those people, remember this: you are not only depleting your critical thinking skills on non-initiative tasks but are also robbing someone else of an opportunity to learn and feel that sense of pride when the task is completed.

Perhaps this type of "I got it" behavior is driven by our inner perfectionist who needs that sense of control over the quality and timing of the task. Or maybe it's our natural sense of empathy, reacting to the discomfort of watching someone else struggle. Whatever our rationale may be, babysitting someone else's monkey is not allowed. Our success and theirs depend on it.

And yes, I know you can do it all. I've seen people do it and have tried it myself on more than one occasion. But the truth is, you can't do it all *and* achieve exceptional outcomes. If we don't consciously set the conditions for the mind to perform at its best, we will continue to feel swamped and, frankly, even a little resentful. Protecting your time from the vampires at the door is essential, even if it means leaving the house through the window.

It's important to recognize that life isn't likely to slow

down on its own anytime soon. Not with those big goals you are going after. But with a little work, you can transform yourself into someone like Neo from *The Matrix*, dodging all the time-sucking distractions speeding at you, staying focused on what matters most. Doing so will ensure that you better slice and dice your precious hours and plug your productivity leaks, choosing the activities that will receive your full attention.

Be sure you are scheduling time to think and creating the space to generate insights that will drive your highest-impact initiatives forward. Say goodbye to constant distractions and back-to-back meetings; do, delegate, or delete tasks as needed so you can drive record-breaking results. The more you practice making these weekly choices, the better you will get at recognizing what does (and doesn't) bring you further time, money, and joy. After all, the brain is your greatest competitive advantage. Setting up the conditions for it to operate at peak levels can be the difference between breaking down and breaking through.

DEEPENING THE WORK

....

KEY TAKEAWAYS

- The brain has only so much energy to perform at its best, and that energy lasts for about four hours a day. Those 240 minutes must be regarded as a priceless treasure.

- You mustn't neglect one of your most fruitful activities: deep thinking. For the ultra-successful, this is not a luxury; it's a necessity. Create those moments for epiphanies to occur.

- You probably think you can multitask, but you can't do so effectively when the activity requires conscious thinking.

- A crucial element of optimal efficiency is managing the usual distractions and time-killers, such as our phones and office interruptions. Manage distractions before they manage you.

- Beware of babysitting other people's monkeys.

EXPLORATORY QUESTIONS

1. More effort doesn't necessarily equate to stronger performance or greater productivity. In fact, working longer hours can make it harder for us to manage our reactions and read one another's social cues. How would you describe the volume of work you are managing both personally and professionally?

2. Does your current schedule give you the time and space you need to be highly effective and productive? If not, what needs to change?

3. What have you been taking on that isn't driving a great deal of value or fulfillment?

4. Where in your life do you need to be asking for help?

TASKS

1. Explore where you could create further capacity for yourself at work and at home by delegating, deferring, or deleting the task entirely.

2. Notice any rationalizations or resistance that shows up as you work to remove things from your calendar. What habitual patterns or habits are triggered?

Jonathan Johnson, chief executive officer of Overstock.com.

Chapter 5

FROM BLIND SPOTS TO BREAKTHROUGHS

CEOs and leaders have to be lifelong students.
Not just students in the sense of attending courses
or reading a book. You've gotta learn how
to read widely, walk the market, look at the trends
in the marketplace, make connections that don't
seem obvious. And start to paint a picture
of what the future could be.
—INDRA NOOYI, CEO OF PEPSICO

....

BREAKTHROUGH PERFORMANCE strategist Price Pritchett tells the story of a fly that keeps hitting a window. Its goal? To get back outside where it can flourish. Ten feet away from the window is an open door, but rather than exploring other possible avenues of escape, it remains convinced that the only way *out* is *through*.[1] So it keeps ramming its head into the glass, again, and again, and again.

How many times have you watched this frustrating melodrama-in-miniature play out for a fly—or on a bigger stage for someone in your life? The truth is, it happens to all of us. Our decisions are only as good as the information they're based on. Those who achieve extraordinary results use curiosity just as much as conviction. Trying harder is not the answer when it comes to exceptional outcomes. To maximize our effectiveness, we need to gain the widest vantage point we can, seeking information that is lurking just outside of view.

....

We need to gain the widest vantage point we can, seeking information that is lurking just outside of view.

....

I called Jonathan Johnson, CEO of Overstock.com, to talk about how he strategically seeks information to overcome his own cognitive blind spots.

---

1 Price Pritchett, *You²: A High-Velocity Formula for Multiplying Your Personal Effectiveness*, https://www.pritchettnet.com/digitalbook/you2/samplebook.php.

FROM BLIND SPOTS TO BREAKTHROUGHS

"When I first became CEO, it was important for me to walk in ready to admit that I didn't know what I didn't know, rather than trying to have all the answers," he explained. "Right out of the gate, I focused on listening and learning and was careful in meetings not to monopolize the mic. 'What do you think?' became the most important question in my repertoire."

Jonathan's approach highlights a clear distinction between *seeking to understand* and *standing to be understood*. The former helped Jonathan and his team open the dialogue around what had to change to transform the company. Their approach paid off as Overstock.com grew from −20 percent to +120 percent revenue in under a year. I watched as he consciously balanced advocacy and inquiry, advocating for his perspectives while listening from a place of curiosity and, perhaps most importantly, admitting when he was wrong.

This may seem like common sense, but it's certainly not common practice. How often have you heard someone start a disagreement with, "Seriously, I'm the one who is wrong here; you are absolutely right!" Rarely, I'd bet, if ever. It goes against our human nature.

That's because admitting you are wrong leads to physical discomfort. For our ancestors, it was thought to make us socially vulnerable and put us at risk of a lower status in the community. But solving the complex challenges of today requires courage and intellectual humility, leaning into that discomfort to pressure test our perspectives and beliefs. When you feel that sense of resistance to an idea, push on to make sure you didn't just trip the wire of a cognitive bias.

"Not seeing what others see can put my decision-making at a disadvantage," shared Jonathan. "I walk into every conversation knowing that I may be missing something, so I ask questions and listen more than I talk. I keep one of those little rubber hammers on my desk—the kind the doctor uses to test your reflexes—to remind myself not to make knee-jerk reactions. If you really listen, it's amazing what you can learn."

We've all watched spy thrillers in which the masterful plan of an experienced team, armed with high-tech gadgetry, goes off the rails because they hadn't done their homework. Overconfident and underprepared, they didn't realize the supervillain had a Rottweiler until it bit them in the ass. This being a Hollywood confection, our heroes improvise, take out their target, and are clinking glasses on the rooftop by midnight, laughing about the dog's weakness for jerky.

In the real world, however, those who achieve exceptional outcomes don't just assume they are right and hope for the best. They step back to see the bigger picture, expanding their view until the fastest route possible to their goal is finally revealed.

ALL THE WORLD'S A STAGE

My client Kevin is an entrepreneur who wears running shoes to work and plays his guitar at the office. He's a salt-of-the-earth kind of guy who can inspire anyone to do just about anything . . . until he gets up on a stage. When the lights turn on and all eyes are on him, he doesn't exactly shine in the spotlight, and that's saying it kindly.

Kevin said yes to media opportunities, keynotes, and conference engagements. He knew he wasn't a song-and-dance kind of man, but he didn't see the business implications of that shortcoming—until one large potential client saw him speak at a conference and moved on to a different supplier within the week.

CHOOSING GREATNESS

The potential client was candid when Kevin called to ask about their decision. "We understand your strategy and, frankly, we liked the team. We just needed to know that our provider had the confidence and capability to deliver, and the other supplier was better able to demonstrate that."

Kevin was shocked. "Give me a break," he said to me. "Not confident and capable? That's a slap in the face. We provide incredible services to our clients."

"Whether you have good services or not isn't the issue," I said. "They were all in before the conference, and then they got cold feet. The problem may not be your skills or your capabilities in delivering services, Kevin, but the behavior you exhibit onstage."

We decided to watch a video of the presentation together, and by the end, he had some observations. "I noticed that I shifted back and forth on my feet. And I could have been better at making eye contact with the audience," he said. "And I definitely could have done a better job at projecting my voice."

"If you saw someone onstage shifting around, not making eye contact, reading the slides, and quietly speaking into the mic, what could you assume about that person?" I asked.

Kevin's eyes widened. He finally got it. His loss of a potential client helped him see a missing piece of information. Kevin had been chopping down a tree with a butter knife, hoping it would one day become an axe. Now he was armed with the insight he needed to drive change.

WHY BAD DECISIONS HAPPEN TO GOOD PEOPLE

Intelligence offers no immunity against bias. That's because the conscious mind can interpret only forty to fifty bits of data per second with roughly eleven million bits coming in.[2] This leaves us with giant holes in our understanding; therein lies the origin of our cognitive biases. Instead of slowing down to seek missing information, we err on the side of speed over accuracy and use our preexisting knowledge, experiences, and beliefs to color between the lines. In other words, in the absence of information, we make stuff up.

We are all more easily duped than we want to believe, even though we are the ones doing the duping. You instant

2 "Understanding Unconscious Bias," NPR, July 15, 2020, https://www.npr
.org/2020/07/14/891140598/understanding-unconscious-bias.

CHOOSING GREATNESS

message a colleague who doesn't reply, and you assume they must be upset. You anticipate an argument, and your more aggressive stance only triggers further disagreement. You believe extroverted people sell best and pass up on hiring a more talented introvert. On a business trip to Las Vegas, you walk past the roulette table and notice your lucky number has hit twice in the past ten rounds. So you drop a hundred bucks on six, even though the likelihood of winning is still 37 to 1.

The brain contains many cognitive booby traps that can come out of nowhere and ensnare our best thinking. The best way to counteract our tendency to make assumptions is to step back and ask meaningful questions:

- What am I missing?
- What else could be true?
- What other possibilities are available?

The last question challenges our automatic bias to move toward binary decisions. Binary thinking is often favorable from our brain's perspective because it quickly generates a sense of certainty, saving our neurological resources for other tasks. For example, if I asked you a binary question—such as whether you would recommend watching *Forrest Gump* to a friend—your brain will automatically migrate to a yes or no answer without much thought. However, if I asked you which part of the movie you think your friend would enjoy the most, your binary bias would be disrupted. This more complex question would elicit a different response and would get your wheels turning in a much more meaningful manner.

We need to be cautious of the gravitational pull toward binary outlooks of this or that, yes or no, right or

> **The brain contains many cognitive booby traps that can come out of nowhere and ensnare our best thinking.**

wrong, my side or your side. That assumes that one of the two options is better when, perhaps, neither option is well thought-out, both can be achieved, or something else is possible! To truly expand our thinking and interrupt our natural biases, we need to move past black and white to explore the whole rainbow of options available.

LEVERAGING THE INSIGHTS OF OTHERS

Kim Rivera.

One of the richest sources of data we can use to gather information is the feedback of others. I asked Kim Rivera how she went about cultivating information to make well-balanced decisions, as she has served as chief legal officer at OneTrust and other C-suite business executive and board director roles at companies such as Hewlett- Packard Inc., DaVita, and Thompson Reuters.

As a diverse female leader, Kim intuitively understands the importance of diversity in thinking and has seen firsthand how it's a gap for many leaders and organizations. As she rose to the highest ranks in her profession, she not only made sure her voice was heard but also placed a high value on listening to the voices of others.

"When you get to a more senior level, it's not about being the smartest person in the room; it's about driving innovation and elevating the entire team," Kim shared.

FROM BLIND SPOTS TO BREAKTHROUGHS

"To be effective you have to disrupt status quo thinking. That requires actively engaging people who are seeing things and doing things differently. Think of it this way: If you are the coach of a basketball team, you're not going to go out on the court and play every position. That's not how it works. Your job is to figure out how to leverage all the vantage points on the court so you can win the game."

When soliciting opinions, we naturally listen to the loudest voices, but we also need to pan for gold in the silences. Who hasn't spoken up? Why? What do they have to say? And be sure to find those who don't think about things the same way you do. Leaning on others with

We naturally listen to the loudest voices, but we also need to pan for gold in the silences.

similar mindsets is like building your own personal echo chamber; you'll end up hearing your ideas repeated back, only to find yourself agreeing.

Whatever goal you are looking to accomplish, critical information can come in the form of the cold logic of a spreadsheet, the obscure musings of a philosophy book, or the knowledge, ideas, and insights of others. It's important to fight the urge to cast a small net in shallow water. If we're going to get objective perspectives, to quote the movie *Jaws*, "We're going to need a bigger boat."

CANDOR REVEALS OUR BLIND SPOTS

Kim also seeks out feedback from others on a consistent basis to make sure she is showing up in a way that's aligned with the outcomes she's driving toward. "I want to know if there is something I could be doing more effectively," she explained. "I ask not just those I have strong relationships with but also those with whom I've had friction or who have a more removed perspective. When you step back and look at the totality of the comments, it's harder to bend the data in your favor and rationalize things away."

There are several ways to gather feedback effectively. You can run a comprehensive 360 feedback review, ask an external individual to facilitate the process, or simply ask a few questions of those you work with or know:

"What do you see as my strengths?"

"Where am I struggling?"

FROM BLIND SPOTS TO BREAKTHROUGHS

"What am I missing?"

"What pattern do you see me repeating that's getting in my way?"

"What advice do you have for me as I continue to grow?"

"I get my own set of formal feedback every year and tell the employees in the company what I am working on," shared Jonathan Johnson. "The more consciously aware I am of how I am coming across, the better I can adjust as I go. When I get feedback, I really look at it. While our natural reaction is to think that it isn't true, over time, I have learned that even misperceptions generally have some truth to them."

Gathering feedback from others is like giving them a giant highlighter to circle whichever actions they believe aren't doing you any favors. Armed with this information, you can then decide when to pull a behavior out of rotation and replace it with something new.

PERSPECTIVES FROM FURTHER AFIELD

To have breakthrough insights, we also need a steady flow of information from outside our bubble. The healthier the diet of information provided, the better the quality of our thinking will be.

It can even be beneficial to seek information that isn't immediately germane to the type of work you do. Doing so expands our ability to think more broadly and avoid tunnel vision. It's this spirit that drives Jonathan to kick off his day with a surprising ritual.

"I read a poem every morning," he says. "I am a naturally analytical person, and this more creative element unlocks a different part of my mind before I get down to business. Even in indirect ways, it can help me empathize more with others and spark ideas around solutions for problems I'm working to solve."

In our modern world of podcasts, documentaries, and books in a wide variety of formats, we have no excuse not to be information treasure hunters. Seek out insights in unexpected places, and you may just find the missing link you needed all along.

How did things turn out for my client Kevin? In short, he used the feedback wisely and got serious about public speaking. We determined how he wanted to look onstage—confident, trustworthy, and world-class in his field. Then, we honed in on the behaviors that would help him get there: filling the stage, making eye contact, and projecting his voice strongly. We videotaped all our rehearsals so he could review them, like an athlete after a match, to analyze his body language.

All that work paid off. Kevin's onstage posture went from "retiring singer- songwriter" to "rock star front man" . . . or at least lead guitarist.

> **Seek out insights in unexpected places, and you may just find the missing link you needed all along.**

Repeating the same behavior over and over and expecting different results is, as the cliché goes, the definition of insanity. Some may find that assessment a little harsh, but at the very least, it's an ineffective strategy. We need to constantly step back to see what we might be missing, look to others for insights, and put our egos aside to properly assess our own thinking. Otherwise, we can end up banging our heads against the window, unable to break through to where greater success awaits.

We end up being the fly.

DEEPENING THE WORK

KEY TAKEAWAYS

- Your brain is hardwired with ancient cognitive biases. Pressure test your opinions regularly to ensure your interpretation of the data is as accurate as possible.

- Look for resistance in your thinking, and be sure to ask yourself why that resistance is there.

- Your choices will only be as good as the data they're based on. Garbage in, garbage out. Make sure you have a healthy stream of information and insights coming in.

- Feedback on your performance from fellow stakeholders is powerful. Be sure to engage those who think differently.

- When soliciting feedback, ask pointed, well-defined questions. This generates better data and outcomes.

- Harvesting big ideas from top minds on a wide variety of topics outside your immediate realm of concern exercises your mind and leads to surprising connections and valuable insights.

EXPLORATORY QUESTIONS

1. Let's identify your strengths. Following is a list of fifty examples; which six words are most reflective of who you are as a person?

Accountable
Adaptable
Analytical
Authentic
Confident
Courageous
Creative
Curious
Delegating
Detail-oriented
Determined
Developing others
Disciplined
Driven
Empathetic
Energized
Enthusiastic

Even-keeled
Experienced
Genuine
Good listener
Flexible
Fun
Hardworking
Innovative
Inspiring
Loyal
Loving
Methodical
Motivated
Open-minded
Optimistic
Organized
Passionate
Patient

Persuasive
Positive mindset
Problem solver
Reflective
Reliable
Relationship builder
Responsive
Resourceful
Storyteller
Strategic
Team-oriented
Thoughtful
Transparent
Trustworthy
Visionary

2. From your perspective, why are those six behaviors so meaningful and important?

3. Conversely, what two behaviors could derail your success or slow down your progress, getting in your own way? Hint: these likely show up when you are under stress of overwhelmed.

TASKS

1. Ask three people you trust what strengths they would highlight when describing you to others. From their perspective, why are those strengths so meaningful and important? Give the person time to reflect on the answer by sending the questions in advance.

2. Ask those same three people what two behaviors they believe could be holding you back or eroding your progress.

3. Spend thirty minutes writing what you've learned through this process.

    a. What are the differences or the similarities between your responses and theirs?

    b. What surprised you or pleased you about the words people used?

    c. What are you now more aware of?

PART 3

CHOOSING A WINNING MINDSET

Daniel Nestor, professional Canadian doubles tennis player.
PHOTO CREDIT: RICH LINLEY - CAMERASPORT

Chapter 6

NEGATIVE REACTIONS TO POSITIVE ACTIONS

Sometimes you climb the mountain, and you fall and fail. Maybe there is a different path that will take you up. Sometimes a different mountain.

—CATERINA FAKE, CEO AND COFOUNDER OF FLICKR

....

DANIEL NESTOR is the most decorated and successful doubles tennis player in history, with an Olympic gold medal around his neck and ninety-one titles to his name. I reached out to Daniel because I wanted to understand what we can learn about insecurities and limiting beliefs in the world of sports and to pull those insights into a business environment. How does he keep negative thoughts at bay when concentrating on something important—like a high-stakes tennis match?

CHOOSING GREATNESS

"At a Grand Slam, I can't afford to go through a swing of emotions," Daniel shared from his home in Toronto, Canada. "Growing up, I had always heard that the game of tennis was 90 percent mental. To me, that sounded ridiculous! I believed that winning and losing matches was dependent on how good you were at hitting the ball."

Over time, Daniel learned that mastering the mental side of the game was essential for peak performance. "When my body wasn't responding the way I wanted it to, or when something was bothering me—too windy, too hot, too humid—I didn't want to let it distract me. My goal was to take the emotions out of it and play with a consistent, almost robotic approach. That was a huge advantage for me against my opponents."

At the highest levels of sport, those who can gain dominion over their negative emotions are the ones who walk off the court as champions. This is a lesson we can also apply to other areas of life. Science tells us that every time you feed a negative emotion, you burn unnecessary mental energy and shift your focus to the crummy way you feel—and away from achieving your goal. As our energy churns in a downward emotional spiral, little is left to lift us up or propel us forward. The more we focus on our negative emotions, the stronger those neural connections become, allowing negativity to get an increasingly powerful hold until it eventually threatens to pull us under.

Think of the psychological sting you feel after saying something you wish you hadn't said or the mountain of pressure before a big presentation. When we shift our atten-

....

Those who can gain dominion over their negative emotions are the ones who walk off the court as champions.

....

tion toward these automatic emotional reactions, we move from goal-directed behavior to self-protection, putting our creativity and problem-solving skills on hold. Simply put, negative emotions are the enemy of growth and high performance, whether you're on the court or in the boardroom.

It's not that world-class achievers enjoy mistakes and difficult moments any more than the rest of us; they simply choose to engage with them differently. Like Daniel, they understand that setbacks and frustrations are just part of the game, and they have go-to strategies for managing them effectively. This allows them to use the mind as effectively as possible, maximizing their ability to drive gains without getting distracted by setbacks.

In this chapter, I'll walk you through three techniques to help you short-circuit negative thinking. By choosing to rewire your defense mechanisms, adjust your mindset around mistakes, and establish a positive talk track, you'll be able to compete like a champion too—no matter the opponent or terrain.

REWIRE YOUR DEFENSE MECHANISMS

Thanks to evolution, our brains are hardwired to avoid risk and discomfort. While this served us well when our primary concerns were finding food, water, and shelter, it has now become an obstacle to personal and professional growth. Our unconscious mind acts quickly, negatively framing anything that can be perceived as a risk and erring on the side of caution. After all, ancient optimists who imagined a rustling in the dark to be just a fluffy bunny didn't tend to have offspring! We are quick to jump to negative conclusions even when we have incomplete information. Consider the following interpretations of neutral events:

- "My client didn't email me back right away. She must be upset about our last conversation." Another possibility? She was running on a tight deadline and couldn't pause to respond.

- "My boss gave me tough feedback. He must think I'm failing at this." Another possibility? He believes in you so much that he's giving you insights on how to grow.

- "Either that team doesn't know what they are doing, or they are intentionally undermining us on this project." Another possibility? They have been given a different directive by their boss, and there is misalignment at the top.

When a perceived risk surfaces, it trips a wire in the brain that activates our defense mechanisms, helping us cope with the perceived rejection, fear, or stress. Most of these defense mechanisms are unconscious emotional shields we don't even realize we're employing. The problem is that defense mechanisms lead to cognitive distortion that insulates us from uncomfortable experiences. We react automatically by

- retreating
- avoiding
- rationalizing
- blaming
- arguing
- defending our position, and
- talking to others rather than the person at the heart of it all.

These tactics can fire without us even consciously knowing, preventing us from truly understanding the situation, learning from it, and moving forward.

Take my client Jill, for example. She is a bright, gifted leader, and her larger-than-life personality makes her easy to work with and an inspiration to follow. She always believed she'd grab the top spot one day and was promoted to her dream job as CEO of a publicly traded company. Six weeks in, the honeymoon phase abruptly ended in her first meeting with the company's board of directors.

"Your strategy is weak, Jill. It isn't aggressive enough,"

one board member said. "You're missing critical steps to drive the level of growth that's expected. At this rate, you aren't going to achieve 15 percent; you'd be lucky to get 10."

Other board members chimed in with their concerns, leaving Jill reeling after the meeting. She slunk away to lick her wounds, and I met with her two days later.

> **Defense mechanisms are unconscious emotional shields we don't even realize we're employing.**

"That was brutal," Jill told me. "Embarrassing. Belittling. Clearly, they missed the point of the entire plan. I'm starting to wonder if they think they made a mistake in hiring me."

Jill was reacting emotionally, which is understandable. But in doing so, she was missing the critically important elements that were included in the feedback. She was mistakenly interpreting a frank assessment of the business strategy as an expression of regret over hiring her. Jill protected herself with a well-worn defense mechanism

("Clearly, they don't understand my strategy!"), and her emotional response was blinding her to the value of the board's feedback.

This is a common experience. We habitually conflate something we *did* wrong with something *being* wrong with us. We suddenly feel like we aren't good enough or smart enough. We feel like we're not worthy of our position. Our stomach churns, our throat swells, our heart races. We struggle to stay afloat in the wash of intense emotion, and we lose sight of the horizon. When this happens, it's essential to recognize and interrupt this pattern before the negative emotions take hold.

I needed to help Jill short-circuit her thinking. "Jill, nothing in here says you shouldn't be CEO," I said, holding up a copy of the board's feedback. "The facts tell me a different story. Do you know what I see here? I see a board that is hyperfocused on fine-tuning your strategy so you and your team can finish the year winning. They dissected your game plan and found places where you need to tighten your approach. While the delivery may have been poorly executed, this is a road map, not a warning letter."

Jill didn't need to hole up in bed, claim they didn't

understand, or beat herself up. She needed to figure out how to move past her defense mechanism and turn to face the feedback head-on.

And that's exactly what she did. After a coaching session focused on unlocking the rich insights contained within the board's feedback, Jill and her team spent the

> **We habitually conflate something we *did* wrong with something *being* wrong with us.**

following three months refining their value proposition, communication strategy, and sales approach—and drove an astounding 18 percent growth that year.

Short-circuiting your defense mechanisms isn't easy, but it is straightforward. Be vigilant about spotting your habitual reactions (most people have two or three go-to defenses) and realizing how they are skewing your view of reality in the moment. When you recognize that you're stuck in one of those defensive grooves, as Jill was, take a moment to breathe and sit in the discomfort. Allow the emotions and adrenaline to move through you before making any big decisions. You can hold discomfort and inquiry at the same time, letting the emotions flow and not reacting to them. Instead, ask questions and really *listen*, giving yourself space to reanchor to the goal of the conversation. The key is to counteract your brain's automatic reaction by accepting the emotion while refusing to give in and respond from that place.

ERASE TERROR FROM ERROR

The second technique to move past your risk-averse brain patterns is to reframe your understanding of mistakes. There's nothing we remember better than a mistake. Think of a time when you were 100 percent confident you were right and acted accordingly . . . only to check your notes later and realize you were 100 percent wrong. Or the time you misread the room, misinterpreted the point, said the wrong thing or had a thought but didn't share it. We relive all those cringe-inducing moments again and again in our minds.

When we mess up, we feel social rejection, and that feeling activates the same region of the brain that responds to physical pain.[1] To your brain, screwing up in a presentation isn't all that different from stubbing your toe or breaking a bone, depending on the magnitude of the error.

It makes evolutionary sense. Eons ago, pain of any kind was a warning signal to stop what we were doing, get to safety, and tend to a wound that might cause our untimely demise. Well, losing status or upsetting others was indeed a threat to our survival and of the utmost concern. If we feel we have done something that may cause people to reject us, that ancient neural wiring fires a warning signal, activating the same pain centers that warn us of physical injury. This reaction is not merely psychological but *physiological*—so much so that taking a Tylenol can make you feel better![2] (While an interesting fact, this is definitely not something I would recommend!) The social pain response is like a mega-habit that has been carved into our brains by hundreds of thousands of years of natural selection.

In this day and age, setbacks are rarely a threat to our survival. Mistakes, when responded to properly, will

---

1 "Study Illuminates the 'Pain' of Social Rejection," ScienceDaily, March 30, 2011, www.sciencedaily.com/releases/2011/03/110328151726.htm.

2 C. Nathan Dewall et al., "Acetaminophen Reduces Social Pain: Behavioral and Neural Evidence," *Psychological Science* 21, no. 7 (July 2010): 931–37, https://pubmed.ncbi.nlm.nih.gov/20548058/.

actually make us smarter, stronger, and better equipped to navigate what's yet to come. Framing your errors as something you can learn from can lead to improved performance on your next swing. This technique is known as *positive error framing*, and studies have linked it to increased levels of performance and quality of output.[3]

Tennis champ Daniel Nestor mastered this approach by looking at every action as nothing more than data to be dissected, a little parcel of essential information to open. If the ball went in the net, he would quickly assess what had to change, make the adjustment, and move on. To maintain focus and interrupt those automatic habitual patterns of negativity, he used cue words for every shot: "Keep your eye on the ball all the way through impact" or "Clean hits anywhere in the court." These were statements he consistently made internally, reanchoring on what was important and moving on to the next point.

We need to strip failures of their emotional power. Actions at work aren't good or bad; they're just effective or ineffective. When an error is made, quickly perform a

3 Debra Steele-Johnson and Zachary T. Kalinoski, "Error Framing Effects on Performance: Cognitive, Motivational, and Affective Pathways," *Journal of Psychology* 148, no. 1 (January–February 2014): 93–111, https://pubmed.ncbi.nlm.nih .gov/24617273/.

mini autopsy to gather information that will inform your next approach. Maybe you'll discover your communication was faulty. Maybe just one little step in the sequence you followed didn't work out. Or maybe you simply faced down the equivalent of a 130-mph monster serve that Daniel Nestor himself wouldn't be able to return, and there is nothing to do but get ready for the next one.

Yes, the discomfort will come, and I'm not suggesting you ignore it. Just recognize that the sting is only a sensation; a neurological and biochemical reaction to the fear of rejection, just like the ache in our lungs after a sprint or the burn of our muscles after lifting weights. Allow yourself to experience it, label it, and then move on. You might say, "Thank you for worrying, but I am all good. I know I can do this." Find the framing that works for you. Don't dive too deep into the waters of negative emotions. There's no need to ascribe more meaning to errors than they deserve.

I called Dr. David Rock to explore the neurological effects that negative thinking can have on performance. "When we focus on the error too long, it sends us into a downward spiral," he explained. "The brain starts to notice more things you don't think you're doing well. It becomes attuned to the error as a threat, and you start retreating. Then your field of view shuts down, perception shuts down, and you make more errors because of it."

A positive relationship to our less-than-perfect moments, an honest release of the unrealistic expectation

....

There's no need to ascribe more meaning to errors than they deserve.

....

of perfection, is one of the key avenues to engaging the world more authentically, more confidently, and better informed. On a neurological level, it provides fertile soil for your brain to grow and creates new neural pathways that expand your problem-solving capabilities.[4]

Choosing to put space between you and your emotions allows you to get an objective view of your experience. Cultivating that arm's-length relationship breaks down their power, allowing the negativity to move

---

4 Jo Boaler, "Mistakes 'Grow' Your Brain," YouCubed, https://www.pdst.ie/sites/default/files/Mistakes-Grow-Your-Brain-Revised.pdf.

through you faster so you can get on with analyzing and adjusting, transforming your next serve from a double fault to an ace.

MAKE A GREATEST HITS
TALK-TRACK PLAYLIST

The final technique to short-circuit your brain's negative wiring involves talking to yourself. Yes, I'm serious. Let's talk about those talk tracks you have running in your mind.

Many people mistakenly believe that being ultra-critical of themselves drives their best performance, but scientific evidence thoroughly debunks this "tough self-love" myth. The last two decades have seen an explosion of insights into how the narrative in our head affects the way we perform.[5] It turns out that what we say to ourselves internally is a significant predictor of performance. In one study, researchers found that athletes who won medals at the 2000 Summer Olympics were more likely than nonmedalists to have used a positive,

5 Joachim Bervoets, "Exploring the Relationships between Flow, Mindfulness, & Self-Talk: A Correlational Study," *Semantic Scholar*, 2013, https://www.semanticscholar.org/paper/Exploring-the-relationships-between-flow%2C-%26-%3A-a-Bervoets/c52c638de8162c6c9ba07c4e3058553f70950b04.

encouraging inner dialogue during competition, and this ultimately led to triumph.[6]

Many of us have grown up being hard on ourselves when we put in a suboptimal performance, internally directing negative language like an angry parent scolding a child. I think somewhere along the line we equated this behavior as being a way to drive performance. But this approach can elicit highly debilitating emotions like guilt and shame—emotional responses that are well-documented as having the power to decrease self-confidence, hinder subsequent performance, and prevent goal attainment.[7]

As a younger player, Daniel Nestor struggled with a tendency to beat himself up over mistakes. His negative self-talk would take his focus away from the game to how frustrated he was feeling about his performance. It was only when he learned to control the voice in his head and shift his attention from himself to his behaviors that

---

6 Marc Taylor, Daniel Gould, and Cristina C. Rolo, "Performance Strategies of US Olympians in Practice and Competition," *High Ability Studies* 19, no. 1 (2008): 19–36, https://www.researchgate.net/publication/234113600_Performance _strategies_of_US_Olympians_in_practice_and_competition.

7 Simon M. Rice et al., "Athlete Experiences of Shame and Guilt: Initial Psychometric Properties of the Athletic Perception of Performance Scale within Junior Elite Cricketers," *Frontiers in Psychology* 12, no. 581914 (April 21, 2021), https://www.frontiersin.org/articles/10.3389/fpsyg.2021.581914/full.

he rose into the upper echelons of tennis.

"No matter what, you will constantly be talking to yourself when you are out there on the court," Daniel explained. "Why not choose to say something constructive? For instance, if I miss a forehand return, I no longer say to myself, *I can't believe I just missed that!* or *That was such a big point you just lost, you idiot!* Instead, I developed the mentality of just accepting it and saying, *OK, I missed that shot. Why did I miss that? What do I need to do differently?* Then I would focus on what has to be fixed. Listen, I'm going to make mistakes, and I'm not in control of whether my opponent hits a great shot on a big point. I just need to regroup and get ready for the next one. Eventually, you realize that to win matches, you can't expect to hit only winners. You don't win tournaments that way. You have to be prepared to deal with the tough times, and how you move through those times determines your end result."

Mindfulness, meditation, and cognitive behavioral therapy are three of many techniques that can help us notice our habitual, repetitive, and negative self-talk—without automatically listening to or acting on it. I recommend trying these methods to help yourself identify and change your talk tracks. The rule I tell my clients to observe is this: if it isn't something you'd say to a friend dealing with tough times, it isn't something you should say internally. Be kind to yourself, moving through errors with ease and grace.

No matter how much external validation you receive, if you don't work on your internal script, you will constantly make yourself feel less than. Only you know how negative the internal monologue running in your head really is, and only you can change the narrative. Become more fully conscious of which song is playing on repeat. Is it "Beautiful Day" by U2 or "Here Comes the Rain Again" by Eurythmics? Choose to drop the depressing teenage angst records into the Goodwill box and move on. It's time to embed a better song in your head, an inspirational power anthem that will pump you up as you drive toward a new horizon, a song that will help you set aside your negative emotions, choose growth, and deliver your very own Grand Slam.

DEEPENING THE WORK

....

KEY TAKEAWAYS

- Tens of thousands of years of programming have created the instinct to focus your mental energy on negative messages over positive ones. This saved your ancestors from predators with sharp teeth, but it doesn't do you any favors in a video conference.

- When you allow your negative emotions to lead, you can freeze up, deplete your energy, and diminish your creativity and problem-solving skills.

- By breaking down the defense mechanisms you've used since childhood, you can make better choices, think more clearly, and enjoy greater success.

- Your distress is a prehistoric reaction to the fear of social rejection. Stop fearing errors, and treat them as the learning opportunities they are.

- The brain doesn't distinguish between physical pain and the emotional pain that comes with making a mistake.

- Analyze what didn't work, isolate what you have control over, adjust your approach, and take another swing. There's no need to make it mean anything about you as a person.

- Self-talk is a proven practice to keep yourself focused on your next action. Build awareness of the soundtrack in your head and continually write more positive lyrics.

EXPLORATORY QUESTIONS

- Negative emotions are as natural and essential as the sunrise. The goal is not to eliminate these feelings but rather govern their amplitude, control their influence, and examine what they are telling us with the healthy skepticism of a scientist. Where is fear showing up in relation to work?

- Where could fear, doubt, or insecurity be holding you back?

TASKS

1. Be on the lookout for when your thoughts shift from goal-directed behavior to self-protection or self-doubt. Your job is not to eliminate this safety instinct; evolution is in charge of that. Observe your fears when they surface, and look for a counter perspective that is equally valid. Now choose which

one will best serve your growth and progression, and focus your attention and effort there! Write the positive belief on paper, post it somewhere you can see it, say it again and again in your mind, tell a close friend, and look for the evidence that backs it up. You are worthy; you are capable; you are exceptional. And there are a million moments to validate that this is true.

2. Acknowledge setbacks and engage with them as nothing more than information—they are an inherent part of the process. With compassion and grace, acknowledge the learning and be kind to yourself; the sting will pass. Smile, breathe through the sting, and know you are better informed now than you were previously. It can be helpful to have a list of five things you can do to move yourself through the pain that can surface with setbacks. Music, time with friends and family, exercise, walks, meditation, journaling, lots of hugs, getting out into nature, whatever it may be—have a go-to list to pull out when it's needed.

Teena Piccione, Global Transformation
and Operations executive at Google.

Chapter 7

NAVIGATING THE RAPIDS OF CHANGE

Don't be intimidated by what you don't know.
That can be your greatest strength and ensure
that you do things differently from everyone else.
—SARA BLAKELY, FOUNDER AND *CEO* OF SPANX

....

"GROWING UP, we had a two-bedroom house for five of us," shared Teena Piccione, Global Transformation and Operations executive at Google. "When you do the math, it doesn't work out! I grew up without a penny to my name. But it really has shown me that we have the power to change whatever path we think we're on."

Teena is no stranger to change. Her life story took her from that two-bedroom home to working with Steve Jobs, consulting at the White House, and leading transformation at one of the largest and most well-known companies in the world, Google. What fuels her fire?

"There are 86,400 seconds available to you every day," shared Teena. "That's it. We are all given the same amount of time, not a second more. How I utilize those seconds to the best of my abilities will create the legacy I live with. I even put that number on all my kids' things because I want them to be intentional around what they choose to do with that time."

Growth requires constant change and adaptation. While this can be exciting and is of critical importance, it is also pretty darn hard. The brain is wired to seek out patterns and predictability and can process uncertainty in the same way it does an error.[1] That's why change can make us feel so anxious and worried, with thoughts ricocheting around, jumping from one risk to the next. One fascinating (albeit ethically questionable) study found that participants who were hooked up to electrodes and told with certainty they would receive an electric shock were less stressed than those in the experiment who were told that the electric

---

1 Felicia Jackson, Brady D. Nelson, and Greg Hajcak, "The Uncertainty of Errors: Intolerance of Uncertainty Is Associated with Error-Related Brain Activity," *Biological Psychology* 113 (January 2016): 52–58, https://psycnet.apa.org /record/2015-58359-008.

shocks *might* happen.[2] Even if predictability isn't pleasant, it somehow feels safer and a little more secure.

To make the most of our time on this planet, we can't let the brain's fear of change derail us. After all, everything is constantly shifting, and if we don't shift with it, our work

....

We can't let the brain's fear of change derail us.

....

can quickly become obsolete. Identify where in your life you want to see change and embrace it, holding that discomfort along with curiosity and conviction. Perhaps you are struggling with work, seeking a career change, frustrated with a project, feeling burned out, or wanting more wealth for the energy you are investing. To change the status quo, choose to adapt your approach and get ready for an exhilarating ride!

THE WINDS OF CHANGE

The first thing to recognize is that change is a process, not an event. Knowing where change is needed doesn't

---

2 "Uncertainty Can Cause More Stress Than Inevitable Pain," ScienceDaily, March 29, 2016, https://www.sciencedaily.com/releases/2016/03/160329101037.htm.

suddenly shift the world on a dime. Otherwise, 70 percent of change initiatives wouldn't fail.[3] While the decision may happen instantaneously, change itself involves moving through the following five-stage process:

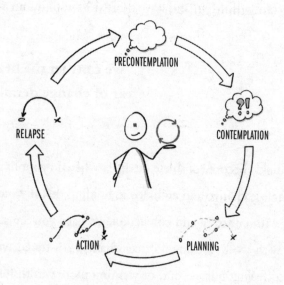

Stage one is *precontemplation*. At this stage, we are unaware or unwilling to accept that change is needed. We may insist that our current circumstances are "just fine," thank you very much. They don't require change, or we don't believe change is possible. There's often a silent hope

3 Nitin Nohria and Michael Beer, "Cracking the Code of Change," *Harvard Business Review*, May–June 2000, https://hbr.org/2000/05/cracking-the-code-of-change.

that the discomfort will resolve on its own.

This grin-and-bear-it approach eventually runs its course, and we shift to *contemplation*. Here, the need to change begins to stir within us. We realize the benefit of doing something differently and start listing out the pros and cons, running through our mental calculators to assess the options and their probability of success. Although we don't have a clear vision of the specific changes we need to make, the haze has started lifting.

This is when we begin stage three, *planning*, where we've accepted the fact that the external shifts require internal adjustments. We map out what's needed to get toward that ever-clearer vision of our castle in the sky.

Flush with excitement, we use that plan to move forward and shift into *action*. This is the "shit is getting real" stage. We've reached a point where we reject this notion of being stuck and have tipped the scales from deliberating to doing.

But wait, there is one more stage that is often overlooked: *relapse*. At times, especially when under stress, we stumble backward and revert to our old behaviors. This is a natural part of the process. While it's true that "fortune favors the bold," we mustn't forget that when we first learned to walk, we fell—a lot.

All too often when we experience this type of setback, we quickly conflate it with failure. "I knew it wouldn't work!" one might say, or "See? I was right, this

....

We mustn't forget that when we first learned to walk, we fell—a lot.

....

was a stupid idea." We need to accept and expect that setbacks are a natural part of the process. Sure, in the movies, when a hero leaps off a bridge onto a getaway van with no training, they can somehow stick a perfect landing. But in the real world, when people attempt a jump like that, it most often ends with a *splat*.

"I frequently hit setbacks," explained Teena. "But I keep going because I know that I am the one creating my own destiny. No one is there to dictate what will happen next but me."

Exceptionally high achievers such as Teena fall just as much as the rest of us. One might argue they fall even harder and more often because they take on bigger goals with higher risks. Regardless, the highest performers are quick to adjust their sails to the changing winds. They choose change, leaning into growth to develop a new set of opportunities and an upgraded status quo.

WHEN SUCCESS BRINGS FAILURE

Sometimes it isn't a failure that brings about the need for change—it's success. Susan was a client who ran operations for a software telehealth platform that blossomed during the COVID-19 crisis. The business took off after widespread shutdowns turned in-person visits into online appointments, almost overnight. The company's sales skyrocketed, and Susan's team couldn't keep up. Her staff was quickly stretched thin as they took on more and more work, scrambling to adapt to the explosive overnight growth.

Susan called me for help in developing a plan to navigate the changes they were experiencing. We arranged an all-day, in-person visit—which, given the pandemic, involved masks, plexiglass barriers, and everyone sitting six feet apart.

I started the meeting with a simple question: "How would you collectively describe what this team's been through over the past twelve months?" Some participants turned their eyes downward, and others looked up at the ceiling. A gentleman in the back let out a big sigh. Clearly no one was feeling energized enough to run toward the type of change that was needed.

Those who had the courage to speak up described a state of overwhelm, confusion, and sheer exhaustion. The collective negativity was palpable and getting thicker by the moment. This type of tension can halt a team's progress, leaving them disconnected, disenfranchised, and dead tired. When we're in this triggered state, we're less able to think objectively and creatively, and we spend more time deliberating over how we feel than focusing on what to do next. Their energy was more of an anchor than a propeller, and I decided to introduce a new question for the team to think through in order to clear the air.

"What do you as a team want to be remembered for?"

Their eyes looked up, and after a few moments, someone decided to chime in. Then there was another. And another after that. The energy and excitement started to build as a new collage of words emerged:

"A team that cares deeply for each other."

"Changing patients' lives for the better."

NAVIGATING THE RAPIDS OF CHANGE

"Making health care more accessible to all."

As the energy shifted, the change they desired began slowly materializing right in front of them. They were mobilizing themselves to find a better way forward.

The remainder of the day was spent on just that—working through a revised strategy that could help them turn the intensity of the wind into an opportunity for advancement, setting sail toward a bigger, brighter future, together.

FRAMING THE PROBLEM AS A QUESTION

When embarking on a quest for change, it's important to make sure the new direction will address the original need or problem. To do this, it can be helpful to accurately identify the issue or opportunity into a clearly framed question. A well-framed question triggers curiosity, helping people push the boundaries on the status quo. For example:

Problem Statement: The sales cycle stalled after a news report about a security breach on our e-commerce platform.

Question: How can we make our customers feel secure about shopping on our site again?

Problem Statement: My presentations come across as average because I don't have time to prepare.

Question: What do I need to do differently to show up so well prepared that I knock my audience's socks off?

Questions are most effective when they are twenty-five words or fewer. This clear framing helps drive focused thinking. Otherwise, we can easily get lost down one

....   •

**A well-framed question triggers
curiosity, helping people push
the boundaries on the status quo.**

....

rabbit hole after another. If there's more than one issue to solve, craft more than one question, and pressure test the quality of each by asking, "If I answer this question, will the issue be resolved or improved?"

Be sure the questions are big and bold, stretching your ambitions and pushing you a little further than you thought possible. If you are going to go through the discomfort of change, you might as well go for it! As Richard Branson shared in our conversation, "Don't be afraid to take that leap into the unknown. The brave may not live forever, but the cautious do not live at all."

THE ART OF CURIOSITY

As with any significant change, learning to adapt to a new behavior or mindset is often a source of psychological discomfort and mental resistance. As we work through the change

....

The brave may not live forever, but the cautious do not live at all.

....

process, we can sometimes feel irritable, down, or drained.

The design firm IDEO created a mood meter to illustrate this point, showcasing how moods ebb and flow during the learning and creation process.[4] When a new idea strikes, hope surges as the work begins! Then, our spirits can dip as we delve into the tedious mechanics of figuring it all out. And finally, as the clouds clear and the

---

4 Sandy Speicher, "The Best Business Breakthroughs Come from Moments of Doubt," IDEO, July 23, 2019, https://www.ideo.com/journal/the-best-business -breakthroughs-come-from-moments-of-doubt.

answer is now obvious, we emerge feeling victorious, with a solution in hand. With this awareness in mind, we need to get off the emotional roller coaster.

"When you are feeling down, just focus on pushing through the next twenty-four hours," Richard told me. "The next day, you will probably wonder why you were feeling so bad about it all! I might get down for a few hours, but then I put it behind me and push on."

Another way to snap out of the downward dips is to frame the entire process as a learning opportunity.[5] This inherently helps us understand that we will experience setbacks and not necessarily know the answer right away. Having this mental flexibility can leave us feeling more confident about letting curiosity off its leash to go sniff around and make some new discoveries.

Richard frequently leverages curiosity as a way to expand his vantage point and figure out what he might be missing. "I love asking questions," he shared. "That's why I take a notebook with me everywhere. To be successful, you can't just hear the sound of your own voice; you have

---

5 Heidi Grant and Carol S. Dweck, "Clarifying Achievement Goals and Their Impact," *Journal of Personality and Social Psychology* 85, no. 3 (2003): 541–53, https://psycnet.apa.org/record/2003-07329-012.

to constantly expand what you know by asking questions."

When we were kids, this part was easy. Children are the ultimate truth seekers, indulging their curiosity with a thousand *why this* or *why that* questions a day. Unfortunately, maintaining that youthful curiosity as grown-ups is not child's play. Our brains are now stuffed with data that's amassed over a lifetime, making us less inclined to invest time in finding new solutions to our problems. By approaching change with humility and an insatiable curiosity, we begin to realize that only one thing is certain: we still have more to learn.

CELEBRATING WINS

As we change, we need to celebrate even the smallest wins and let dopamine do its thing. Highlighting wins is extremely beneficial, letting the brain know this is one go-to sequence of behaviors we will want to repeat!

My client Susan's team had committed to doing just that during the workshop, sharing appreciation and gratitude freely. Six months later, the team was humming. Together, they had clearly identified the four key measures for the team's success, eliminated or consolidated low value-add meetings, right-sized their teams to become more agile, and focused on fostering a highly connected and caring culture. At around that time, I got a call from the CEO of the company, who invited me to join Susan and her team for dinner to celebrate their undeniable progress.

After arriving at the restaurant, I said my hellos and took my seat beside Susan. The group settled in, and the CEO stood up, asking for everyone's attention.

"Susan," he said, smiling in her direction, "I want to recognize the incredible efforts you and your team have made." Susan's husband and daughter then walked into the restaurant and sat down at the end of the table. Clearly this was a surprise to Susan, whose eyes were darting back and forth, trying to figure out what was going on. The CEO smiled and continued.

"This team's results have been outstanding," he said, "and Susan, your leadership has been nothing short of inspirational. I invited everyone here tonight so they could shake your hand in person—as our newest executive vice president. We would be honored and lucky to have you as part of the senior leadership team." The table erupted into applause, and Susan's daughter ran over and fell into her arms, eyes welling up with emotion.

Driving exceptional outcomes requires the courage to lean in and choose change. This is your life. Your story. What changes are you seeking?

"Every person on this planet was created to be extraordinary," shared Teena. "When you were born, the doctor didn't look down and say, 'Nah, you're not very good; you're on Team B.' Instead, everyone looked and smiled, knowing that you were someone special."

If we start from the understanding that you are exceptional, that you are special, that you are worthy, then you need not worry about the uncertainty that comes with

....

This is your life. Your story.
What changes are you seeking?

....

the shifting currents and changing tides. Trust yourself to find a way. Hold the discomfort and curiosity simultaneously, knowing that those sensations don't need to drive your behavior. Instead, step out of the boat, analyze what's going on, adjust your approach, and get right back into action, making the most of today's 86,400 seconds.

DEEPENING THE WORK

KEY TAKEAWAYS

- In this fast-paced, rapidly evolving world, success requires us to rely on our ability to adapt quickly.

- Change is a process, not an event! It doesn't happen automatically and may or may not be linear. No judgment required.

- Remember that changing a behavior or mindset can bring about short-term psychological discomfort. You can feel that discomfort and still choose the behavior or thought that will drive you toward your goals.

EXPLORATORY QUESTIONS

1. How comfortable are you when faced with the need to change?

2. When you are upset about or resisting change, what behaviors tend to show up?

3. What changes in your personal or professional life feel a little intimidating right now?

4. What positive benefits exist on the other side of those changes?

TASKS

1. It can be helpful to break a big change into smaller chunks, cutting the monster of a problem down to size so you're not fighting with its giant illusory shadow cast on the wall. Pick a change you are either currently experiencing or looking to generate. What small actions can you take to get started?

2. Where in your life do you find yourself complaining? What change is needed here? Yes, there is a time and space for venting; we just need to make sure we aren't getting ourselves stuck in a state of focusing on our dissatisfaction for too long. The more complaining we do, the more we divert our focus away from the change that's needed to how we feel about the situation itself.

Kim Rivera, chief legal and business affairs officer at OneTrust.

Chapter 8

CRUSHING IT WITH CONFIDENCE

*I've been absolutely terrified every moment of my life—
and I've never let it keep me from doing
a single thing I wanted to do.*
—GEORGIA O'KEEFFE, ARTIST

....

KIM RIVERA's energy electrifies the room, lighting people up with her big ideas and bold sense of determination. Nothing seems too challenging to tackle, no issue too hard to resolve. I find myself leaving every conversation a little better off than I was before.

After losing her parents at fifteen, Kim was faced with a stark reality. "I had little money, limited resources, and lived in a community with no clear opportunities for advancement," she shared as we spoke. "Instead, I had to envision a future that seemed impossible and will it into existence, putting every ounce of energy I had into making it happen."

Kim told me about the way she had to take risks, leaping without a safety net, inherently needing to believe in her own abilities to stick the landing. "There was no time to worry what other people were thinking of me," she shared. "I knew that I couldn't let my emotions override my ability to achieve forward momentum. The best thing I could do was to get out of my neighborhood and get a good education, carving a different path. And no, I didn't always have the right answer or see what the right next step was to take. But I trusted myself to figure it out, never taking my eye off what I wanted to do next."

Kim put herself through Duke University and Harvard Law School, then became an attorney, rising to the highest ranks in her field as a chief legal officer, and then on to other C-suite business executive and board director roles at companies such as DaVita, Hewlett-Packard Inc., Thompson Reuters, and OneTrust.

Having this type of grounded sense of self can have an immeasurable impact on your career, multiplying your level of effectiveness in any given engagement. Research has shown that confidence boosts performance by increasing our efforts, enhancing our resilience, and improving our overall mood.[1] One study found that participants raised their scores on an IQ test as much as ten points simply by recalling a time when they drove a successful outcome.[2]

Confidence not only influences how we perform but also attracts others, like a lighthouse in the fog. People seek out those they trust to steer the ship in the right direction because it reassures them that someone knows the way. In fact, the brain's reward system is often activated around confident people,[3] producing biochemical reactions in relation to that grounded sense of certainty.

For those of us looking to cultivate our own sense of confidence, the good news is that it's a skill, not a trait. We can put more swagger in our step, regardless of what

1 See Kate Hays, Owen Thomas, Ian Maynard, and Mark Bawden, "The Role of Confidence in World-Class Sport Performance," *Journal of Sports Sciences* 27, no. 11 (2009): 1185–99, doi: 10.1080/02640410903089798; and A. Bandura, "Self -Efficacy: Toward a Unifying Theory of Behaviour Change," *Psychological Review* 84 (1977): 191–215.

2 "Self-Worth Boosts Ability to Overcome Poverty," UBC News, December 17, 2013, https://news.ubc.ca/2013/12/17/self-worth-boosts-ability-to-overcome-poverty/.

3 "How Our Brains Are Biologically Tuned to Be Influenced by Confident People," *Neuroscience News*, December 13, 2016, https://neurosciencenews.com /confident-people-neuroscience-5734/.

our DNA is doing. Let's explore some evidence-based strategies to get there.

SHAKING HANDS WITH YOUR INNER CRITIC

Many of us are taken by the illusion that confident people feel confident all the time, like 007 in every James Bond movie. Because of this illusion, we end up seeing doubtful thoughts as a weakness or a failure. The truth is that anyone who says they've eliminated self-doubt is selling you snake oil.

"It's not that I am not afraid," shared Kim. "Because sometimes I am and question what in the world I think I'm doing! I still have doubts, but I work on building the fortitude to carry the fear and anxiety differently—knowing it's there but not letting it stop me from moving forward."

Doubt is a universal neurological safety mechanism that's triggered when we step—or even *think* of stepping—outside our comfort zone. It helps us go into situations with our eyes wide open, further scrutinizing information and acting as a barometer for risk.[4] It also keeps us grounded so we don't venture off into overconfidence

4 Therese Huston, "How Self-Doubt Can Actually Help You Make Decisions," *TIME*, August 8, 2016, https://time.com/4432856/self-doubt-decisions/.

or arrogance, when we see ourselves as superior to others versus comfortable in our own skin. (Interesting to note, both arrogance and narcissism stem from deep insecurities rather than an inflated sense of self.[5])

You see? Doubt has an important job to do in keeping us balanced! Its role, however, is not to predict the future; it's merely a test run of hypotheticals, a dress rehearsal to iron out what could go wrong before the curtain goes up.

The problem is, as we saw in chapter 2, the brain doesn't

....

Doubt is a universal neurological safety mechanism that's triggered when we step—or even *think* of stepping—outside our comfort zone.

....

easily distinguish between thoughts that are real or imagined. When we watch a horror movie, for example, we irrationally wonder for a fleeting moment if someone is hiding behind

5 See Nelson Cowan et al., "Foundations of Arrogance: A Broad Survey and Framework for Research," *Review of General Psychology* 23, no. 4 (December 2019): 425–43, https://www.ncbi.nlm.nih.gov/pmc/articles/PMC8101990/; and "Narcissism Driven by Insecurity, Not Grandiose Sense of Self, New Psychological Research Shows," New York University, March 25, 2021, https://www.nyu.edu/about/news -publications/news/2021/march/narcissism-driven-by-insecurity--not-grandiose -sense-of-self--ne.html.

the couch or about to call us from inside the house. Of course, the mind trick is more obvious, and we shift to our go-to strategies of turning on a comedy or calling a friend.

Thoughts of self-doubt are nothing more than scary stories of another sort. Managing these thoughts requires choosing your own repertoire of interventions. Here are a few evidence-based suggestions for those times when self-doubt is getting the upper hand:

- Make time for light exercise to rid your mind of anxious energy.[6]

- Create a kick-ass playlist to get you fired up for moments when you need it the most.[7]

- Call a friend to get your mojo moving.

- Pull a "compassionate U-turn" to flip your mindset around by writing yourself a letter or saying the words of affirmation and support you need to hear.[8]

---

6 Timothy J. Schoenfeld et al., "Physical Exercise Prevents Stress-Induced Activation of Granule Neurons and Enhances Local Inhibitory Mechanisms in the Dentate Gyrus," *Journal of Neuroscience* 33, no. 18 (May 1, 2013): 7770–77, https://www.jneurosci.org/content/33/18/7770.

7 "Music and Health," *Harvard Health Publishing,* September 11, 2021, https://www.health.harvard.edu/newsletter_article/music-and-health.

8 "Compassionate U-Turn," The Centre for Compassion Inspired Health, March 9, 2021, https://compassioninspiredhealth.com/2021/03/09/compassionate-u-turn/.

- Take action on a task to feel a sense of control and progress.

- Label the thoughts as nothing more than fleeting opinions, reframing them into something more useful and positive.

- Engage professional support and build your own list of strategies to turn the volume down on self-doubt.

- Most importantly, avoid making decisions when doubt is in the driver's seat. It's there to consult, not run the show.

"In life, I spend a lot of time monitoring my emotional state to make sure that I'm standing on solid ground," Kim explained. "I am consistently scanning to see how I feel—whether I am mad, tired, disappointed, or frustrated—to make sure that those emotions aren't affecting my thinking and judgment. If I am experiencing an intense emotion, I think through how I can address it besides just resting. Who can I call to get a reality check, and what would my decisions look like if I was making them from a healthy place right now?"

CHOOSING GREATNESS

By understanding the impermanence and limitations of doubt, we can choose not to succumb to its seduction, stopping it from silently eroding our confidence by understanding its benefits and overall intent.

ENVY: THE ULTIMATE CONFIDENCE KILLER

One of the most common ways we erode our self-confidence

....

By understanding the impermanence and limitations of doubt, we can choose not to succumb to its seduction.

....

is by comparing our progress with that of others. Research has found we are hardwired to see the world in terms of hierarchy, with a decrease in perceived social positioning and status activating the brain's emotional pain circuitry.[9] This inclination to peek over the fence at our neighbor's backyard is an innate reaction forged through eons of tribal existence. In prehistoric times, those who were higher in

---

9 "Human Brain Appears 'Hard-Wired' for Hierarchy," National Institutes of Health, News Releases, April 23, 2008, https://www.nih.gov/news-events /news-releases/human-brain-appears-hard-wired-hierarchy.

the pecking order of a group were rewarded with more resources. This type of in-group comparison mattered to our survival and ability to thrive.[10] That's potentially why we feel more envy toward those we know rather than toward Beyoncé or Bill Gates.

But the pecking order at the watering hole mattered much more in our hunter-gatherer days. Today we can all dip our toes into a larger global pool of opportunity; modern life doesn't need to be a zero-sum game.

"I respect and admire people for what they are able to do," Kim shared. "I celebrate their achievements and

> **Today we can all dip our toes into a larger global pool of opportunity; modern life doesn't need to be a zero-sum game.**

help others wherever I can. But I don't let myself think for one second that they are better than me. I can honor the accomplishments of others without giving some type of undue deference."

10 Vilayanur S. Ramachandran and Baland Jalal, "The Evolutionary Psychology of Envy and Jealousy," *Frontiers in Psychology* 8, no. 1619, September 19, 2017, https://pubmed.ncbi.nlm.nih.gov/28970815/.

CHOOSING GREATNESS

When envy surfaces, it can be useful to try the following:

- **Detach the desired object or outcome from the individual who achieved it**—in reality, envy has nothing to do with the person at hand.

- **Pay the individual a compliment** and lean in with compassion and gratitude, both wonderful antidotes to envy.

- **Step back and look at the bigger picture** so you don't get tunnel vision and lose sight of your own growth and wins. The object of envy may or may not be a path you are interested in pursuing.

- **Maintain distance** from the object of envy if it's derailing your own sense of self. Research has shown that space and time have wonderful benefits in decreasing this emotion.[11]

- **Reframe the desired object or outcome as a goal.** In this way envy can be a tool for self-improvement when—and only when—it's beneficial to do so.

When you find yourself wanting what others have or feeling you could do what others have done

---

11 A. C. Kristal, E. O'Brien, and E. M. Caruso, "Yesterday's News: A Temporal Discontinuity in the Sting of Inferiority," *Psychological Science* 30, no. 5 (May 2019): 643–56, https://pubmed.ncbi.nlm.nih.gov/30958730/.

(and better!), remember that this is nothing more than a neurological response. Sit in the discomfort and let it pass, using the strategies above, and recognize that someone else's win doesn't offset your own success story.

PROGRESS OVER PERFECTION

Self-confidence is built through practice and requires setting aside our perfectionist tendencies. You know the ones I mean, the deep-rooted desires to perform without errors, to hit it out of the park with every swing. But striving for *excellence* and striving for *perfection* are not one and the same. The former focuses on high standards and continuous learning to enhance our outcomes. The latter sees any deviation from excellence as a failure.[12] That's why perfectionist tendencies *decrease* creativity and performance,[13] shifting our efforts from the goal to the risks and leaving us playing *not to lose* rather than playing all out *to win*.

"I don't know anybody in life who has achieved great

12 Joseph Junewick and Richard B. Gunderman, "The Perils of Perfectionism," *American Journal of Roentgenology 213,* October 2019, https://www.ajronline.org /doi/pdf/10.2214/AJR.19.21158.

13 Beth Ellwood, "Study Suggests That Striving for Excellence—but Not Perfection—Boosts Creative Performance," PsyPost, June 14, 2022, https://www.psypost .org/2022/06/study-suggests-that-striving-for-excellence-but-not-perfection-boosts -creative-performance-63325.

success by playing it safe and doing all the right things," Kim shared. "Driving exceptional outcomes doesn't come with being tidy and predictable."

Our desires for perfection often stem from child-hood experiences in which we incorrectly came up with the concept of "They will love me if I . . ." That faulty

....

Our desires for perfection often stem from childhood experiences in which we incorrectly came up with the concept of "They will love me if I . . ."

....

childhood belief is not serving us well in the here and now. There is no "if" when it comes to self-acceptance.

All too often we assume that a pat on the back will be the key to enhancing our sense of self-worth. We wait for it, perform for it, hoping that just as we do our best work, someone will be watching. But the only one watching you perform every day is the one looking back in the mirror. It's time to start providing her or him with the praise and posi-tivity needed to crush through goals and feel the drive and energy of a champion. And yes, undoubtedly, for all of us, when we receive validation, feel-good chemicals are released by our brain, providing a quick reward and reinforcing the experience. But our sense of self is only temporarily elevated, if at all. Many high achievers I work with seek validation but have a hard time hearing it when it comes, cautiously listening for the word *but* to follow. Remember, self-assuredness is an internal process, not an external one. And the only person who can stoke that fire is you.

Instead of seeking perfection and the validation of others, frame each task as a learning opportunity, accepting yourself regardless of how it goes. With that progress-oriented mentality, each day we can actively take more risks, pushing harder and farther while continuing to grow. Each small step accumulates, driving exponentially more progress over time. And when it matters most, you will have more skills and awareness to not only hit the ball out of the park but to knock it out of this hemisphere.

FIRST IMPRESSIONS ARE REAL

When you walk into a room, what level of confidence and competence are you projecting? It turns out that we as humans are constantly taking mental snapshots of the way others show up, quickly forming impressions of their overall capabilities and character. This is known as "thin slicing," where the brain saves neurological resources by making quick decisions based on limited information.[14] The most powerful pictures captured are those of our nonverbal body language. And as they say, a picture is worth a thousand words.

In one fascinating study, participants were instructed to watch videos of a piano competition and asked to pick out the winner.[15] Clearly, it would take an expert ear to determine who among the pianists played best, yet inexperienced participants could accurately identify the winner 47 percent of the time. The real kicker? In one scenario, the videos had no sound. Yes, you read that right. The participants predicted the winner accurately just by how the musicians carried themselves onstage.

Here are some techniques to consistently present yourself as a maestro of confidence:

- Pull your shoulders back and down. All too often they end up somewhere near our earlobes, sending

14 Michael W. Kraus and Dacher Keltner, "Signs of Socioeconomic Status: A Thin-Slicing Approach," *Psychological Science* 20, no. 1 (2009): 99–106, https://journals.sagepub.com/doi/abs/10.1111/j.1467-9280.2008.02251.x.

15 Chia-Jung Tsay, "Sight over Sound in the Judgment of Music Performance," *PNAS* 110, no. 36 (2013): 14580–85, https://psycnet.apa.org/record/2013-31888-005.

the message that we are stressed out with no time to engage.

- Sit up straight, even on video conferencing. A slouched posture telegraphs disinterest or distrust.

- Make eye contact, meeting the gazes of others. Staring at your shoes connotes avoidance, concealment, or timidity.

- Be still and strong in your silence. Frantic fidgeting, leg tapping, or constant jerky motions only amplify nervous energy and put the people in the room on edge.

These are just a few quick techniques, though it can be helpful to determine what you personally look like when showing up at your best. Close your eyes for a moment and envision your most confident self. What do you see? How are you holding your shoulders? Your head? Your arms? Your facial mannerisms? This is the version of yourself that you want to project consistently.

With that vision imprinted in your mind, push your thumb and forefinger together firmly. This subtle action is known as anchoring,[16] an associative conditioning

---

16 Mary R. Thalgott, "Anchoring: A 'Cure' for Epy," *Academic Therapy* 21, no. 3 (1986): 347–52, https://journals.sagepub.com/doi/abs/10.1177/105345128602100314 ?journalCode=iscb.

technique that can provide you with a mental marker in a pinch (pun intended) to bring you back to that image when you need it the most.

In addition to body language, studies have shown that wearing the right clothes can also heighten perceptions of confidence and authority.[17] When we dress to impress, people tend to see us as more persuasive, competent, and trustworthy.[18] In one study, participants were able to negotiate better outcomes when wearing suits instead of sweatpants.[19] In another involving a mock real estate transaction, the suit-and-tie folks negotiated 10 percent more profit than the casually dressed dudes.[20] Choose to wear something that not only makes you feel good but also denotes professionalism in your field. This can vary greatly, depending on whether you spend your days in Silicon Valley, Wall Street, or Main Street.

Human beings are constantly looking for that sense

17 "The Science of Having More Confidence," Hoffeld Group, https://www.hoffeldgroup.com/the-science-of-having-more-confidence/#_ftn3.

18 "Science of Having More Confidence."

19 Ray A. Smith, "Why Dressing for Success Leads to Success," *The Wall Street Journal*, February 21, 2016, https://www.wsj.com/articles/why-dressing-for -success-leads-to-success-1456110340.

20 Yuki Noguchi, "Power Suits: How Dressing for Success at Work Can Pay Off," *Morning Edition*, NPR, March 18, 2016, https://www.npr.org/2016/03/18 /469669877/power-suits-how-dressing-for-success-at-work-can-pay-off.

of certainty that confidence brings; we want to feel that we will make it, that we will get there, that we will be good enough to succeed. But here's the thing. You have already proven that you can overcome unbelievable hardships— not just by getting through tough projects at work but by pulling yourself together after setbacks, getting back on your feet when you fall, and weathering the storms of sadness, fear, and anxiety that blow in from time to time. And here you are, still standing. Those battle scars have proven that you are prepared to take on anything.

The secret to confidence is recognizing that it is already within you. Don't wait for it to surface; cultivate it every day. We need to remember that the only problem with our beliefs is that we believe them! Consciously choose to reinforce those that launch you forward vs hold you back. That way, after slaying your next challenge, you can walk out with that James Bond-like swagger, holding your head up high and reciting these words:

I am worthy of achieving my version of Greatness.

This is my shot.

My turn.

My time.

Roll credits.

DEEPENING THE WORK

··

KEY TAKEAWAYS

- Confidence can be cultivated through conscious choice. While DNA can have an effect on our confidence levels, confidence is a skill, not a trait.

- Self-doubt is not something to be eliminated but to be channeled into greater preparation and focus.

- Confidence is not about perfection; rather, it's about rejecting the negative emotions you feel when you make mistakes, focusing on the lessons learned, and applying them to reach your objectives.

- Let go of the fear of losing face, being wrong, and making mistakes. Redirect your attention once you begin to ruminate.

- The way you carry yourself in physical space dictates how people will react to you, often more than your words. Eye contact (without making it weird) and sitting up straight are good. Fidgeting and fumbling are bad.

- Dress for success. It's not just a saying; it's science.

- Comparing ourselves with others is a natural way to

gauge our success, and to fall into envy is human. We can turn negatives into positives by observing our feelings and choosing to focus on what we can learn from them.

- Life has kicked your butt once or twice, and it will again. You've overcome every test to get where you are, which proves you can take on whatever comes next. You've got this!

EXPLORATORY QUESTIONS

1. Focusing on being perfect is more like an anchor than an engine, weighing you down versus driving you forward. Where are you being overly hard on yourself?

2. Where in life do you feel a great deal of confidence?

3. Where do you tend to struggle with confidence?

4. Whose approval are you often seeking?

5. What are you hoping they will say?

6. How can you go about filling that need internally rather than seeking that external validation?

TASKS

- Make a list of all the things you are proud of in life. Accomplishments, relationships, skills, hardships, setbacks, lessons learned—put it all down on paper!

- Write out what this list means about who you are as a person. Positives only please!

- Share the answers to these exploratory questions and your homework with someone who cares about you. Let them in on the sound of your inner critic along with the things you are proud of in life.

PART 4

CHOOSING MASTERY

Phyllis Yale, advisory partner at Bain & Company.

Chapter 9

COMMUNICATING FOR MAXIMUM IMPACT

Raise your hand, take risks, and don't fear failure –
it's one of the biggest impediments to success.
—CATHY ENGELBERT, FORMER CEO OF DELOITTE

. . . .

HAVE YOU EVER BEEN excited to share an idea in a meeting, only to receive a lackluster reception?

Or had the opportunity to blow the room away with a presentation, but created nothing more than a slight draft?

No matter how towering our intellect or marvelous our sense of humor, when we don't communicate our thoughts effectively, we squander opportunities to bring our ideas to life.

"How I express myself determines the impact I can

have in any given conversation," shared Phyllis Yale, advisory partner at Bain & Company. "Not to mention the likelihood that I'll be invited into the discussions that matter most."

Phyllis is a lifelong student of communication, leveraging these skills to make strides toward her broader goal of changing healthcare for the better. She earned an MBA

....

When we don't communicate our thoughts effectively, we squander opportunities to bring our ideas to life.

....

from Harvard, ran Bain's East Coast operations, and has served on the boards of several Fortune 500 healthcare companies and nonprofit organizations.

But early in her career, Phyllis struggled to communicate her thoughts effectively. She brought me back in time to a meeting where a younger Phyllis was providing an update to senior leaders. "As soon as I started speaking," she shared, "I could feel a surge of emotions. My throat closed, and I was short of breath; I was barely able to get the words out. My colleagues were very nice about the whole thing, but there was an elephant in the room, and that elephant was me."

Phyllis sought out techniques to sharpen her skill set by asking for support, getting feedback from mentors, putting prep time on her calendar, and consistently rehearsing the heck out of things—practices she continues to carry out today. No one would know that this titan in her field had, once upon a time, felt timid. "I always say that I am walking proof that communication is a learned skill," she shared.

Investing in communication will consistently pay dividends, multiplying the impact you can have in any meeting. That's why those who work toward mastering this craft are more likely to emerge as leaders,[1] land that next promotion,[2] advance their careers,[3] and above all, be heard.

---

1 B. Schultz, "Communicative Correlates of Perceived Leaders," *Small Group Behavior* 11, no. 2 (1980): 175–91, https://doi.org/10.1177/104649648001100203.

2 Virginia L. Bean and Judith E. Watanabe, "An Investigation into the Importance of Communication Skills," *Journal of Applied Business Research* 4, no. 4 (1988): 1–6, https://clutejournals.com/index.php/JABR/article/view/6384.

3 Jennifer A. Polack-Wahl, "It Is Time to Stand Up and Communicate," 30th ASEE/IEEE Frontiers in Education Conference, Session F1G, October 18–21, 2000, https://archive.fie-conference.org/fie2000/papers/1084.pdf.

THE PAPER AIRPLANE

In our youth, making paper airplanes was as common an activity for many of us as watching our favorite cartoons. We would meticulously shape the sharp creases to the proper proportion so that with the flick of a wrist, the plane would fly through the air with ease. Getting the tip just right was fundamental to its performance.

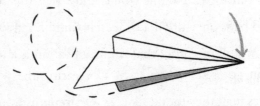

Well, it turns out that communication is quite similar. The first thing you say that hits the air is of the utmost importance, shaping what people hear next and what they will retain.

Let me show you what I mean. In a series of experiments, two groups of participants were given a brief list of adjectives describing an individual.[4] For our purposes, let's call this individual Steve. Group A was told that

---

4 S. E. Asch, "Forming Impressions of Personality," *Journal of Abnormal and Social Psychology* 41 (1946): 258–90.

- Steve is intelligent, industrious, impulsive, critical, stubborn, and envious.

Group B then received the exact description but in reverse order:

- Steve is envious, stubborn, critical, impulsive, industrious, and intelligent.

Participants were subsequently asked to write a short description of Steve's overall character. Which group do you think described Steve more favorably?

You guessed it, Group A. By hearing the positive adjectives first, they found that Steve's strengths overshadowed his shortcomings. Group B, on the other hand, had been primed with the negative adjectives first and believed that Steve struggled with some serious personality flaws!

The respondents were influenced by what's known as the *primacy effect*. This is a type of cognitive bias—a systematic error in our thinking as it relates to memory and attention. What's said first is what we hear next, priming a particular mindset and determining what knowledge and beliefs are activated in one's mind. This bias is so pesky and pervasive that several communication frameworks across various industries have been designed to address it:

- In the military, where ambiguity in the field can lead to confusion and loss of life, they use a framework known as the Bottom-Line Up Front (BLUF).[5] Right out of the gate, the most important piece of information (the bottom line) is placed at the top of the message (up front).

- In the healthcare industry, where 80 percent of medical errors result from miscommunication, healthcare professionals created the SBAR model (Situation, Background, Assessment, Recommendation).[6] This technique removes any room for ambiguity and facilitates the clear and rapid transfer of information between care teams.

- In sales, to spark interest, salespeople hone their "elevator pitch,"[7] distilling their message down to thirty seconds or less—about the duration of an

5 Kabir Sehgal, "How to Write Email with Military Precision," *Harvard Business Review*, November 22, 2016, https://hbr.org/2016/11/how-to-write-email-with-military-precision.

6 Martin Müller et al., "Impact of the Communication and Patient Hand-Off Tool SBAR on Patient Safety: A Systematic Review," *BMJ Open* 8, no. 8 (2018): e022202, https://www.ncbi.nlm.nih.gov/pmc/articles/PMC6112409/.

7 Allison Gaffey, "The Elevator Pitch: How to Craft a Successful Five-Minute Elevator Pitch and Why Having One Is Important," Psychological Service Agenda, June 2014, https://medschool.vanderbilt.edu/wp-content/uploads/sites/9/files /public_files/Psychological%20Science%20Agenda.pdf.

elevator ride with a potential customer.

- In the media, headlines are used to grab the attention of readers and shape the message they will take away. In fact, one series of experiments found participants can read the same article but derive different perspectives simply by changing the headline.[8]

Whatever your industry, condensing your thoughts and starting with the *headline* can be the difference between one that soars and one that nosedives right into the carpet. It needs to be clear enough to highlight the quality of your thinking and crisp enough that people could repeat it if asked when they walk out of the room.

> **Condensing your thoughts and starting with the headline can be the difference between one that soars and one that nosedives right into the carpet.**

8 Ecker, Ullrich K. H., Lewandowsky, Stephan, Chang, Ee Pin and Pillai, Rekha. 2014. "The Effects of Subtle Misinformation in News Headlines," *Journal of Experimental Psychology: Applied*, 20(4), 323–335, https://doi.org/10.1037/xap0000028.

WHAT'S YOUR HEADLINE?

When it comes to communication, structure is critical. Without the right scaffolding, the individual elements will come tumbling down. Studies have shown that a lack of structure decreases our credibility,[9] makes the content hard to retain,[10] and is less appealing to the listener.[11]

"Communications that end in a conclusion aren't nearly as influential as ones that begin with the conclusion up front," shared Phyllis. Be sure to boil your thoughts down into your own concise, well-structured headline so that people don't just listen, but they leap out of their seats!

One of my clients, Kristin, the vice president of sales for a software company, asked me to help prepare her headline for an upcoming leadership meeting. The latest monthly report had seen yet another decline in sales—this one marking the third month in a row for her team. At this rate, she knew their chances of hitting the company's annual targets were quickly eroding. When the CEO asked her to share an update, she needed to be prepared.

---

9 E. E. Baker, "The Immediate Effects of Perceived Speaker Disorganization on Speaker Credibility and Audience Attitude Change in Persuasive Speaking," *Western Speech* 29 (1965): 148–61.

10 E. C. Thompson, "An Experimental Investigation of the Relative Effectiveness of Organizational Structure in Oral Communication," *Southern Speech Journal* 26 (1960): 59–69.

11 R. G. Smith, "An Experimental Study of the Effects of Speech Organization upon Attitudes of College Students," *Speech Monographs* 18 (1951): 292–301.

COMMUNICATING FOR MAXIMUM IMPACT

"What do you need to communicate?" I asked while turning on the audio recorder so we could document her thoughts.

"Our clients are focused more on summer vacation right now, making it difficult to create a sense of urgency," she replied. "Every year, we seem to hit this lull, and our team is doing everything we can to overcome it. But let's face the facts: We are struggling to meet our numbers with our client base disconnected from work right now. The team is putting in a lot of hours and working incredibly hard to generate results, but we can't seem to get our customers' attention to grow our client base and deepen existing customer relationships. There just isn't enough time in the day to do it all. We need to get more strategic and more focused if we are going to address this."

There was a high probability that Kristin would have already lost her audience. She started off with summer vacation; maybe some folks are now thinking about their plans to go to the beach! And we still aren't sure what "struggling" means or what the plan is to turn it around.

How could Kristin frame her communication to be more concise and compelling?

Headline: Sales are declining for the third month in a row, putting our annual targets at risk. We have identified three different strategies to quickly drive growth and turn things around.

Supporting information: Here are the three ways we are going to tackle this.

Let's jump to another client, Vashir, who heads up the HR department for a technology company. Vashir called me after he observed continual turnover in the product department. He structured his headline as follows:

Headline: After reviewing the data, we identified that employees are leaving in their first six months. Refining our onboarding process will have a significant impact on retention.

Supporting information: Here are three changes we can make immediately to enhance our new employee experience.

When it comes to the supporting information, because of the limits of our short-term memory and processing capacity, three points is often the magic number.[12] The rule

---

12 G. A. Miller, "The Magical Number Seven, Plus or Minus Two: Some Limits on Our Capacity for Processing Information," *Psychological Review* 63, no. 2 (1956): 81–97, doi:10.1037/h0043158.

of three is built around the fact that our short-term memory quickly assesses small batches of information before either logging them in or letting them go. Famous examples? "Friends, Romans, countrymen"; "life, liberty, and the pursuit of happiness"; "sex, drugs, and rock and roll." Aim for at least two and no more than four, or just go with the rule of three! For example, you may share three ways you plan to address the problem, or three reasons you believe it's happening, or three risks that need to be addressed.

Whatever the content may be, it's important to stay concise and compelling, keeping your talking points tight to avoid tangents. As the saying goes, be brief, be bright, and be gone. "It is very hard to be compelling if you speak in paragraphs," explains Phyllis. "When you use too many words, you can lose the audience. Speak in bullet points instead."

Being brief helps hold the listener's attention, while additional information often leads us down the proverbial "rabbit holes" that may not even be relevant to the broader topic. While the gap between what you understand about the topic and what the listener understands may be vast, less is often more.

CHOOSING GREATNESS

This isn't just a framework for the most important meetings; every encounter is an opportunity to have an even greater impact. In fact, real decision-making doesn't occur in the boardroom but in those micro-moments throughout the day as people gather data and form their perspectives. I recommend scheduling an hour every week to look ahead and jot down your thoughts for upcoming meetings.

- What is the headline that you need to communicate? Or key question you want to ask?

- What supporting information do they need to know?

That way, you are ready to hit the ground running by the time Monday rolls around.

SPEAK LIKE YOU OWN IT

To effectively influence others, we need to engage in a way that feels more like a firm handshake than a weak tap on the shoulder or a hard punch. That brings us to the three styles of communication, which operate along a spectrum from *passive* to *assertive* to *aggressive*.

COMMUNICATING FOR MAXIMUM IMPACT

On one side of the spectrum, we find a more *passive* communication style. When we use this style, we may come across as too soft or lacking in confidence. What we say can land flat, only to have someone else share it later and be celebrated for their genius.

PASSIVE   ASSERTIVE   AGGRESSIVE

Passive communication often leads to us holding back comments in meetings to avoid being criticized or wasting people's time. When we communicate in a passive manner, we get unintentionally overlooked for our contributions and presence as we engage more actively after the meeting via email or one-on-one discussions.

When we use this style, we may diminish our contributions with caveats such as "I could be wrong here" or "Not sure this is quite right, but . . ." All these actions together decrease the likelihood that our ideas will take flight.

On the other end of the spectrum, we find a more *aggressive* communication style that can come across as too harsh and overbearing. People will likely avoid us when we show up in this way. Even when we are on point, our comments are often negatively perceived because they are cutting through the room like daggers, leaving people ducking for cover rather than wanting to engage.

Aggressive communication can lead to sharp or provocative language. We come at someone like a freight

....

Passive communication often leads to us holding back comments in meetings.

....

train, putting them into an immediate defensive posture. Those leaning on this style tend to interrupt people, present their ideas as facts rather than as opinions, and take up more airtime than is needed. Aggressive communication can shut down productive conversation in an instant.

For the purpose of high-impact communication, both of these styles at the ends of the spectrum can miss the mark. Like *Goldilocks and the Three Bears* (notice the number), one chair is too soft, one chair is too hard, but look—there is one that's just right!

In the middle, we find the *assertive* communication style. This style is concise and compelling, protecting one's own boundaries without overstepping the boundaries of others. No subtext or further explanation required; the message is clear, easy to digest and understand. The assertive approach is also compelling, grabbing the listener's attention with clear purpose and confidence. This is important, because a listener's attention can start to decline sixty seconds into whatever you're saying![13]

Instead of coming at someone, stand shoulder to shoulder, staring at the problem together. When we leverage this style, we project a high degree of objectivity, even in heated discussions. Perhaps that's why supervisors who leverage an assertive style are seen as more trustworthy and are better able to influence decision-making.[14]

13 Diane M. Bunce, Elizabeth A. Flens, and Kelly Y. Neiles, "How Long Can Students Pay Attention in Class? A Study of Student Attention Decline Using Clickers," *Journal of Chemical Education* 87, no. 12 (2010): 1438–43, http://pubs.acs.org/doi/abs/10.1021/ed100409p?journalCode=jceda8.

14 Shilpee Dasgupta, Damodar Suar, and Seema Singh, "Impact of Managerial Communication Styles on Employees' Attitudes and Behaviours," *Employee Relations* 35, no. 2 (December 2012), https://www.researchgate.net/publication/263383632_Impact_of_managerial_communication_styles_on_employees%27_attitudes_and_behaviours.

Bring a sense of optimism, positivity, and hope, even if the message is challenging. If you want people to follow, you need to make sure that you're heading somewhere others will want to go! If sales are down, you wouldn't say,

....

A listener's attention can start to decline sixty seconds into whatever you're saying!

....

"We're going into third quarter behind again, and we can't see a way out of this; it's terrible." People will be more likely to run for the hills than lean in to help you. Instead, one could say, "We're going into third quarter behind; this is our moment to dig in, drive change, and finish the year in the position we all know we are capable of achieving."

Communication is the vehicle for your ideas, the conduit for connections, and a powerful tool for transforming relationships and results. "It's important to be a lifelong learner of this skill," shared Phyllis. "I am constantly observing effective presenters and facilitators to see what works for them, learning and taking notes to this very day!"

COMMUNICATING FOR MAXIMUM IMPACT

Choose to invest every day in how you communicate. Investing in this skill will unquestionably pay dividends, helping you achieve the goals you are after. The infamous rivalry between Nicola Tesla and Thomas Edison comes to mind. As the story goes, Tesla possessed a formidable intellect that might well have overshadowed Edison's, but he often struggled to sell his ideas with the spark required (pun intended).

Bottom line? Be the spark.

DEEPENING THE WORK

KEY TAKEAWAYS

- Communication is a skill that we need to continue to refine throughout our careers.

- Lead with your most important piece of information, the headline, then follow up with the supporting facts.

- Condense your message into two to four key points for optimal processing and retention.

- Structure your message for clarity, jotting down bullet points in advance so your communication is crisp.

- Schedule an hour every week to look ahead at your calendar and jot down your thoughts for your upcoming meetings.

- Which of the three speaking styles do you use the most? Is your default communication style passive, assertive, or aggressive? Working your way to assertiveness will serve you best.

EXPLORATORY QUESTIONS

- When are you most uncomfortable communicating your thoughts?

- What strategies can you use to show up at your best during these situations?

- What strategies or tools have been helpful in the past when it comes to communication?

TASKS

1. When looking at your important meetings next week, prepare one or two questions or thoughts you would like to share. Capture them in bullet point format so you are ready to hit the ground running when Monday rolls around.

2. Identify one communication skill you would like to develop over the next three months and lay out a plan on how to refine that technique.

Everett Thomas, executive at Lockheed Martin,
major general (US Air Force, retired).

Chapter 10

LEVERAGING THE STRENGTH IN NUMBERS

Fight for the things that you care about,
but do it in a way that will lead others to join you.
—*RUTH BADER GINSBURG, SUPREME COURT JUSTICE*

GENERAL EVERETT THOMAS is one of those people you meet whose résumé can stun you into silence, making you wonder how he managed to fit so much service into one career. Everett helped lead the Air Force Global Strike Command and was chief of the Nuclear Arms Control Division, vice commander for the US Air Force Warfare Center, deputy director for Middle East and International Negotiations, survived the 9/11 Pentagon bombing, and was awarded two medals for his contributions to the war on terror. He now serves as an executive at Lockheed Martin Space.

CHOOSING GREATNESS

After spending five minutes with Everett, you quickly realize that he thinks about his accomplishments quite differently than most. As he sees it, his wins belong to the team, not to him. For every yard gained and every point scored, he looks back and sees all the hands and heads that got the ball over the goal line.

Everett and I sat down to talk about the importance of relationships in business. "When I used to speak to those being deployed," he said, "I would share a lesson that I've learned firsthand: You are not alone. Do not be afraid. All your training and experiences have prepared you for this moment. We all face times when we feel overwhelmed with what's in front of us. Remember that the people you have learned from are imprinted in your mind and there by your side. Whatever happens, wherever you are, just know we are in this together."

In some ways, Western civilization has done us a disservice by celebrating a different kind of hero, the kind we entertain ourselves with on Saturday nights. You know the one—the rugged individualist, the independent ass-kicker, the superhero who seeks out injustice and finishes his day on the rooftop alone, the one who thinks needing others is pitiable and that signs of weakness are unwelcome. These lone wolves have been fashioned over millennia and injected with steroids for Hollywood screens. While fun for entertainment purposes, going it alone is a costly real-world strategy.

The modern-day billionaire did not build her empire independently. Nor did the scrappy entrepreneur get through the lean years without engaging his friends. To drive exceptional outcomes, modern-day heroes reach out to their networks, enlist their allies, and build strong connections and communities. In the real world, we learn a lot more from heroes like Everett.

> **Modern-day heroes reach out to their networks, enlist their allies, and build strong connections and communities.**

THE COST OF BEING THE LONE WOLF

Marvin is a marketing executive who is consistently thought to be the smartest person in the room. Yet somehow, his career had flatlined.

CHOOSING GREATNESS

He gave me a call after being passed up for another promotion. Year after year, his feedback was the same: it wasn't what he was doing; it was how he was doing it that was the problem.

Marvin would get frustrated when projects weren't moving rapidly, but he didn't know how to bring people along. He spent most meetings driving the discussion and most nights redoing people's work. This only increased the volume of tasks he was managing, leaving him more connected to his laptop than to his team. Marvin had quickly become a leader without followers.

While rowing a boat alone might sound lovely— no one telling you how to paddle or which way to go, no one dragging down your speed with their crummy rowing technique—your progress is only as strong as your stroke. Now, imagine that same boat suddenly filled with ten skilled rowers. They help navigate tough weather, cover each other for breaks, and pull ten times the water you were managing on your own. Let's face it: the focus on connectivity isn't just about warm and fuzzy feelings; it's about horsepower, exponential achievement, and the breadth of insights required to travel faster and farther while having way more fun getting there.

CONNECTIVITY DRIVES PERFORMANCE

As pack animals, we're hardwired to work better together. With allies around us, research has shown that we take more calculated risks, are less likely to burn out, and persist 64 percent longer when pushing tasks to completion.[1] It's a stark fact that we need each other, not only to be able to take on bigger goals but also to survive. Without human-to-human interaction, we are 50 percent more likely to die prematurely.[2]

Why then do we insist on doing so much ourselves, both at home and at work? How do we address the stigma that asking for help is a bad thing? The superhero mentality that high achievers aspire to can put a ceiling on our success and quietly lead to strong feelings of resentment. The hero in us can sustain only so much weight alone before we get a little irritable and worn out.

---

1 See Murad Hussain, "Effect of Teamwork on Employee Performance," *International Journal of Learning & Development* 1, no. 1 (2011) 110–26; and Adi Gaskell, "New Study Finds That Collaboration Drives Workplace Performance," *Forbes*, June 22, 2017, https://www.forbes.com/sites/adigaskell/2017/06/22/new-study-finds-that-collaboration-drives-workplace-performance/?sh=4a9ccc9b3d02.

2 Julianne Holt-Lunstad, Timothy B. Smith, and J. Bradley Layton, "Social Relationships and Mortality Risk: A Meta-Analytic Review," *PLOS Medicine* 7, no. 7 (2010): e1000316, https://journals.plos.org/plosmedicine/article?id=10.1371/journal.pmed.1000316.

CHOOSING GREATNESS

It's important to slow down at work and intentionally engage with others in a meaningful way. This is particularly true for those of us who work remotely and don't have the chance to walk by the water cooler to catch up with colleagues. Everyone has their own secret world brimming with the magical and the mundane. The energy and interest you bring into discussions will determine how much or how little of that you will get to see.

Also invest time asking substantive second- and third-layer questions beyond the weather and weekend plans so people feel valued, seen, and heard in our

....

The hero in us can sustain only so much weight alone before we get a little irritable and worn out.

....

engagements. Science has shown that how a coworker feels about our connection with them dramatically affects not just the relationship but the effort they bring to the work.

One study really brings this point home. Researchers had participants undergo brain scans while talking about leaders.[3] When asked to discuss leaders with whom they had a positive relationship, fourteen regions of the participant's brain lit up. When asked to discuss leaders with whom they had a negative relationship, six parts of the brain lit up and eleven actually deactivated.

The real insight of this study is to be found in examining which areas switched on and off. Negative relationships activated the regions of the brain that drive self-protective behaviors, turning off those responsible for connection and problem-solving skills. The subjects were more focused on getting away from the leader than helping them win.

I will be the first to admit it can be hard to find the time to build our relationships in such a stressful environment. Our days are often overflowing with obligation and stacked with back-to-back meetings. When we're facing down what feels like a house fire, it can be hard to make time to strike up a conversation with the neighbors. That being said, if we regularly nurture those connections, we may just find those neighbors standing by our side with a bucket of water right when we need it the most.

---

3 Richard Boyatzis, "Neuroscience and Leadership: The Promise of Insights," *Ivey Business Journal*, January/February 2011, https://iveybusinessjournal.com /publication/neuroscience-and-leadership-the-promise-of-insights/.

WHO'S GOT YOUR BACK?

As Everett and I explored the importance of allies, he shared a rather terrifying tale.

He had been tasked with negotiating a reduction in US and Russian strategic nuclear weapon stockpiles. Everett and the delegation flew into Moscow, and the group was immediately debriefed. "When people started to leave," he shared, "they pulled me aside and let me know there was a neo-Nazi convention in town. They were concerned for me as an African American and couldn't guarantee my safety. One of the men I was traveling with was Caucasian and had grown up in Montgomery, Alabama. He chimed in and said, 'Ev, we aren't going to let them get in our way. We're going out tonight and you're coming with us!' The thing about allies is when you need them the most, they find you. Although I *did* ask how fast he could run, recognizing I just had to be a little faster than the next guy!"

One could say Everett was lucky to have friends like that at work. But this had nothing to do with luck; it's the by-product of building compassionate and caring connections. It turns out that consciously investing in relationships with others changes not only the way we engage with the world but also the way the world engages with us.

At this point, you may be wondering, *How strong are my relationships?* Let's stop to take stock of our connections. On a sheet of paper, make a quick list of five people you work with on a regular basis. How would you rate the strength of those relationships on a scale of 1 to 10?

- 10 = Best relationship ever!
- 6 = It's fine; we manage.
- 1 = When I'm working with this person, I want to call an exorcist.

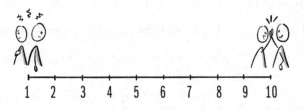

If you rated any of your relationships below a 7 out of 10, it can be beneficial to step back and explore how to invest even further. Is there anything eroding the quality of the connection? What actions could be taken to deepen the trust?

CHOOSING GREATNESS

Taking the time to intentionally reflect on our relationships is a fruitful activity that reaps great rewards. After all, strong relationships at work increase our happiness,[4] boost productivity, decrease job stress,[5] create a sense of belonging,[6] and improve decision-making.[7] The list of tangible benefits is lengthy, giving us good reason to harness our connections to supercharge performance and maximize results.

I feel compelled to share that we also need to watch for those who drain our sense of self and overall energy. Some bring us up, and some bring us down, and it's worth observing interactions to see where those peaks and valleys lie. How can you manage or minimize the interactions with people who zap your energy? I have a CEO client who is highly selective of his interactions

4 Sue Roffey, "Positive Relationships at Work," in *The Wiley Blackwell Handbook of the Psychology of Positivity and Strengths-Based Approaches at Work*, ed. Lindsay G. Oades et al. (New York: John Wiley & Sons, 2016), 171–90.

5 K. T. Tran, P. V. Nguyen, T. T. U. Dang, and T. N. B. Ton, "The Impacts of the High-Quality Workplace Relationships on Job Performance: A Perspective on Staff Nurses in Vietnam," *Behavioral Sciences* 8, no. 12 (November 2018): 109.

6 R. F. Baumeister and M. R. Leary, "The Need to Belong: Desire for Interpersonal Attachments as a Fundamental Human Motivation," *Psychological Bulletin* 117, no. 3 (1995): 497–529.

7 R. Sharda, G. L. Frankwick, and O. Turetken, "Group Knowledge Networks: A Framework and an Implementation," *Information Systems Frontiers* 1 (1999): 221–39, doi: 10.1023/A:1010098227671.

with energy drainers because he's convinced the overall cost he and the team expend in these interactions is greater than any gain he feels the person delivers. At first, such calculations might seem harsh, but I'm not suggesting you be the mob boss driving anyone having a bad day out to the desert for a tough chat. It's just that over time it's okay to shunt your energy away from relationships that bring only negativity and drama. And so, in this way, it isn't only about the relationships you strengthen but also the ones you minimize. There's simply too much to accomplish to be unnecessarily and consistently dragged down by exhausting emotions.

BUILDING SOLID RELATIONSHIPS IS A NUMBERS GAME

Positive relationships at work cause the release of the neurotransmitters dopamine and oxytocin, both for us and for our colleagues.[8] These feel-good hormones not only generate a sense of pleasure, positivity, and attachment but also enhance our health and financial

8 Marcial Losada and Emily Heaphy, "The Role of Positivity and Connectivity in the Performance of Business Teams: A Nonlinear Dynamics Model," *American Behavioral Scientist* 47, no. 6 (2004): 740–65, https://journals.sagepub.com /doi/10.1177/0002764203260208.

success.[9] So how can we optimize relationships to get more hits of that sweet, sweet dopamine?

Research has shown that powerful relationships are built on a ratio of 5:1 positive to negative interactions. This concept originally emerged from research conducted by John Gottman, who could predict the stability of marriages with 80 percent accuracy based on their ratio of positive to negative engagements.[10] Negative interactions might include moments of hostility, defensiveness, criticisms, or leaving someone feeling ignored. Positive interactions might include moments of active listening, showing appreciation, kindness, or laughing together at a joke or silly meme.

Showing appreciation is a particularly powerful tool that can not only strengthen the bond but boost someone else's performance and well-being.[11] It can be helpful to drop a reminder into your calendar twice a week, priming

9 L. J. Brent, S. W. Chang, J. F. Gariépy, and M. L. Platt, "The Neuroethology of Friendship," *Ann. NY Acad. Sci.* 1316, no. 1 (May 2014): 1–17.

10 John M. Gottman, James Coan, Sybil Carrere, and Catherine Swanson, "Predicting Marital Happiness and Stability from Newlywed Interactions," *Journal of Marriage and Family* 60, no. 1 (1998): 5–22, https://doi.org/10.2307/353438.

11 N. S. Fagley, and Mitchel Adler, "Appreciation: A Spiritual Path to Find Value and Meaning in the Workplace," *Journal of Management, Spirituality & Religion* 9, no. 2 (June 1, 2012): 167–87.

the brain to watch for these little opportunities when you can lean in with gratitude. It might be thanking your partner for taking out the trash, a nod to a colleague for getting back to you quickly, or an acknowledgment of your boss's efforts to remove a roadblock. While all connections can't be sunshine and rainbows, driving for more positive touch points will help you forge stronger bonds that withstand the weight of the work.

WHY BEING RIGHT CAN BE WRONG FOR RELATIONSHIPS

We all know on an intellectual level that greatness is never achieved in a vacuum; a leader without followers has no leverage. Sergey Brin and Larry Page may have cofounded Google in their dorm room, but it took an immeasurably vast network of people to bring their innovations to the world. Every bold endeavor, from a scrappy start-up to a vast empire, takes a team of dedicated people working together.

When working with others, we will inevitably come up against conflict. People aren't programmed automatons or, as my kids might say, NPCs—nonplayer characters— in our video game, waiting to hear our commands and executing on cue. There will come a time when you don't see eye to eye with a colleague. This is not a bad thing! Conflict is an incredibly powerful way to strengthen relationships and expand our thinking. Disagreement doesn't have to be a battleground where one party wins and the other walks away feeling scorned. So how can we communicate during conflict in a way that doesn't sever connection?

I'll answer this by sharing the tale of the monkey and the banana. The story goes like this: A trapper goes

....

Conflict is an incredibly powerful way to strengthen relationships and expand our thinking.

....

out into the jungle and puts down a narrowly barred cage that's filled to the brim with bananas. A monkey passing by sees the bananas and reaches his arm in, but because the bars are so close together, he is unable to get the banana out. The monkey keeps pulling, unwilling to let it go, regardless of the approaching trapper who comes out of the jungle and grabs him.

LEVERAGING THE STRENGTH IN NUMBERS

During conflicts, we tend to hang on too tightly to our perspectives and refuse to let go of the banana, even when it's to the detriment of the relationship or outcome. To effectively navigate conflict at work, we need to begin by putting our banana down. That way, we can move objectively into talking through the problem to find the most effective solution.

It can also be useful to start conflict-based discussions with agreement, perhaps agreeing on the overarching goal or on the issue of the conflict itself. That aligns both parties in such a way that they are standing shoulder to shoulder and looking at the problem together rather than coming at each other head-on, as discussed in chapter 9.

During conflict, cognitive biases will rapidly surface since the potential for risk has seemingly increased. For example, when we are unhappy with an individual, we are more likely to see their behavior as intentional and blame-worthy.[12] Even neutral behaviors are often seen in a negative light. It can also be easy to jump to all-or-nothing

---

12 F. D. Fincham and T. N. Bradbury, "Assessing Attributions in Marriage: The Relationship Attribution Measure," *Journal of Personality and Social Psychology* 62 (1992): 457–68. See also William R. Cupach and Daniel J. Canary, "Conflict: Couple Relationships," https://family.jrank.org/pages/312/Conflict-COUPLE -RELATIONSHIPS.html#ixzz7e4NnEIYL .

thinking in which anything the other person says is quickly compartmentalized as either good or bad, right or wrong (in a conflict, their comments often end up in the latter). But between those two ends of the spectrum lies an ocean of opportunities. We are better off exploring the issue objectively so we don't lose sight of the goal and, frankly, the relationship before they both smash into an iceberg.

Connections are critical to our ability to perform and achieve extraordinary feats. Take Marvin, the marketing executive I mentioned earlier in this chapter. Once he began investing in others, listening to their ideas, and demonstrating his genuine sense of appreciation, everything changed. He and his team drove the work together, and their performance took off. Marvin now has a group that would walk over coals to help him succeed—because he, as their partner, would do the same for them.

"When I was a commander of the 341st Space Wing, we had four thousand personnel defending the United States with combat-ready airmen and nuclear forces," shared Everett. "One of the group commanders in the wing was frequently insubordinate behind my back. I would ask him to do something, and he would turn around to his squadrons and tell them he wasn't going to do it. I was quickly informed, and I asked him flat out, 'Colonel, are you working for yourself or the Air Force?' He ended up deciding to step down, and two days before his retirement ceremony, he came to my door upset. His family was coming, and he couldn't find a senior officer to perform the retirement ceremony. He asked if I would help him. Of course, I did, because I believe people are inherently kind. Later in life, when I was the commanding officer at another installation, I came across this same man and his wife, and you know what? He was the first to come over and hug me."

We may prize the lone wolf for their strength and independence, but in today's world, there's no reason to be left pushing the boulder uphill all alone. With a strong team of allies, we're not pushing or pulling—we're *building*, together.

As Everett had said, "You are not alone. Do not be afraid. All of your training and experiences have prepared you for this moment. And when you need an ally, just know we are there by your side."

DEEPENING THE WORK

KEY TAKEAWAYS

- Building your community means you must be as committed to your ally's success as you are to your own.

- Never squander an opportunity to ask meaningful questions and be timely in your communications.

- Take control of the quality of your interactions. The first step is identifying five people who are critical to your success and honestly assessing the strengths of those relationships on a scale of one to ten.

- When someone has a negative view of you, their brain quite literally shuts down, which narrows their attention to focus on their own protection. This is essentially a stick in the spokes of problem-solving and collaboration.

- To build strong connections, remember to shine the spotlight on others, demonstrating a strong sense of appreciation and care.

- None of us can go it alone; everything is optimized when we keep our key relationships strong.

EXPLORATORY QUESTIONS

- How can you prioritize relationships despite a full schedule?

- How do you want to show up with others when you are under stress?

- What could you do to be more present in your current relationships, both at work and at home?

TASKS

- Reflect on three stories about you that you could share with others at work. Write the stories out in bullet points to make sure you can sum it up in two to five minutes.

- Find opportunities to share those stories with others and ask people about their lives as well.

Daniel Nestor.

Richard Branson.

Kim Rivera.

Eric Severson.

Chapter 11

OVERCOMING OVERWHELM

Almost everything will work again
if you unplug it for a few minutes—even you.
—ANNE LAMOTT, WRITER

WHAT'S THE SECRET to high performance that many of
us miss?

"Highly successful people have the same level of
discipline around renewal as they do around the expendi-
ture of energy," shared Eric Severson, the Neiman Marcus
executive you met in chapter 4. "After all, sprinters only
run fast because they rest between sprints. Having discipline in these areas makes us far more successful."

Eric's perspective was echoed by every single leader
I have worked with over two decades who has achieved

extraordinary results. It's not a fluffy, woo-woo idea but a science-backed approach to high performance that requires our full attention.

The longer and harder we work without recharging, the less effective the brain becomes—and we're often too busy to notice. A Stanford study found that those who work more than fifty hours a week saw diminishing returns after their fifty-fifth hour.[1] How can this be? Think of it this way: if you want to build your leg muscles, you wouldn't do squats for twelve hours straight. Clearly, at some point, this overinvestment of effort would do more harm than good.

"I get paid at work to bring my best thinking forward," shared Kim Rivera. "It's important that I manage my day to create the right conditions for that to happen. Otherwise, I hit a point when somebody asks me a question, and I literally draw a blank. That's a clear sign that I've pushed my brain too far."

High achievers tend to have ambitious goals, and the consequences of physical and mental depletion can put those goals at risk. Tasks get rushed, errors occur, concentration suffers, and emotions become raw. Even

1 John Pencavel, "The Productivity of Working Hours," Stanford University and IZA, April 2014, https://docs.iza.org/dp8129.pdf.

when exhausted, it can be hard to fall asleep—or stay asleep! This constellation of symptoms doesn't bode well for productivity, performance, or relationships. Choosing to optimize our regime for the brain to perform at its

....

High achievers tend to have ambitious goals, and the consequences of physical and mental depletion can put those goals at risk.

....

best is perhaps the most important choice we can make. Without it, by the end of the day, our sprint will have slowed down to a crawl.

THE RIPPLE EFFECTS OF RUNNING TOO HARD, TOO LONG

Wendy was the executive medical director for a hospital system. Since the beginning of the pandemic, she had been constantly running as patient loads increased and staffing challenges escalated. Bouncing from meeting to meeting and one crisis to the next, Wendy barely had time to catch her breath.

"It's like I can't turn my brain off," she said when we spoke. Wendy's relentless workload had led to a complete cratering of engagement in the rest of her life. Her husband, John, was feeling the absence, and while she kept saying things would change, the change had never come. One evening, Wendy arrived home to find John waiting at the front door with his suitcase in hand. He kissed her on the cheek and said he loved her dearly, but he was tired of feeling alone. She watched as his car's taillights disappeared down the street and darkness settled in around her.

Wendy had toiled valiantly to juggle all the projects at work, but the ball she cared about most had fallen to the ground and shattered. Our conversation initially cycled around the "should-haves" and "could-haves" as she swirled about in the past exploring what went wrong. These reflections were creating a downward spiral of energy and keeping Wendy from moving forward. We needed to latch on to a vision of what was possible that could pull her out of this muck, and quickly.

"Wendy, what would your ideal future look like?" I asked gently.

OVERCOMING OVERWHELM

Wendy paused, took a deep breath, and began sharing her vision. It was as though she were looking through a portal to another realm, seeing herself move around through the various parts of her life with ease and grace. She and John were laughing, hugging, and present with each other. Work was intense but inspiring, and she had boundaries in place to log off and take breaks. I could feel her energy shift as she anchored to this new future. Was it possible to achieve? For the first time, she was determined to truly figure it out.

THE WEIGHT OF STRESS

Before I lose my skeptics, let me be clear. Recharging is not about chanting with colleagues and taking month-long vacations on a beach (although, if you can pull it off, more power to you). It's not about lighting candles while standing on your head or floating weightless in a sensory-deprivation tank (though both of those sound quite lovely). Recharging is about finding those breaks that interrupt the endless sprint with moments of respite, shifting your focus inward and putting the intensity on pause.

CHOOSING GREATNESS

Let's get back to the science. Recharging involves stimulating your parasympathetic nervous system, which activates the renewal of cells, tissues, and organs, allowing your body to rest and repair.[2] Your muscles relax, your breathing slows, your digestion resumes, and your heart rate decreases. These pauses replenish your attention stores before you can go back out and run again.[3]

Many of us, however, spend most of our time in high gear due to perceived emotional or physical stressors. When the pressures escalate or threats loom, the sympathetic nervous system revs, keeping our senses heightened and body on alert.[4] Our blood pressure increases, digestion slows, and breathing becomes shallow and rapid.

In short bursts, this sympathetic nervous system response is normal—healthy, even. But when stress levels are soaring too high for too long, the effects on our health and mind can be detrimental.

Consider this: In the United States we enjoy one of

---

2 "Parasympathetic Nervous System (PSNS)," Cleveland Clinic, https://myclevelandclinic.org/health/body/23266-parasympathetic-nervous-system-psns.

3 Ferris Jabr, "Why Your Brain Needs More Downtime," *Scientific American*, October 15, 2013, https://www.scientificamerican.com/article/mental-downtime/.

4 "Sympathetic Nervous System (SNS)," Cleveland Clinic, https://my.clevelandclinic.org/health/body/23262-sympathetic-nervous-system-sns-fight-or-flight.

the most advanced healthcare systems in the world. For decades, we've reaped the benefits and experienced longer life expectancies. But in the past five years, American life

....

Recharging is about finding those breaks that interrupt the endless sprint with moments of respite, shifting your focus inward and putting the intensity on pause.

....

expectancy has started to decrease and stress levels have gone through the roof.[5] Given the constant changes in our social, economic, and healthcare environment, people have a heightened level of anxiety around work,[6] the economy,[7] their relationships, and their health.[8]

5 "Life Expectancy in the U.S. Dropped for the Second Year in a Row in 2021," National Center for Health Statistics, August 31, 2022, https://www.cdc.gov/nchs /pressroom/nchs_press_releases/2022/20220831.htm.

6 Carolyn Crist, "Most Americans Report Overwhelming Stress Levels: Poll," WebMD, March 10, 2022, https://www.webmd.com/anxiety-panic/news/20220310 /americans-report-overwhelming-stress-poll.

7 "Stress in America 2020: A National Mental Health Crisis," American Psychological Association, October 2020, https://www.apa.org/news/press/releases/stress/2020 /report-october.

8 "APA: U.S. Adults Report Highest Stress Level since Early Days of the COVID-19 Pandemic," American Psychological Association, February 2, 2021, https://www.apa .org/news/press/releases/2021/02/adults-stress-pandemic.

CHOOSING GREATNESS

The problem is, we often don't see the consequences of our stress-based existence, so we push off getting our proverbial shit together to another day. And so we tolerate the sleepless nights and stress-ridden days, unaware of the consequences on our performance and well-being. Together, we can shift this dynamic by holding each other accountable to take care of ourselves, putting our own oxygen mask on before worrying about the rest of the plane.

"I have a philosophy that I call Circles," Richard Branson shared as we talked about the importance of recharging. "It all starts by drawing a circle around yourself and including everything you need to show up in a way you can be proud of. Exercising, eating the right foods, getting enough sleep. Once you have that circle set up in a way that works, you can draw another circle, then another, then another, as you look after your family, friends, employees, and communities. But it starts by getting yourself in order first."

Self-care is not selfish. Carving out moments in the day to recharge is neither a gift nor a luxury; it's a necessity. Only then will we have the energy to show up at our best and be in service of others. As the saying goes, you can't pour from an empty cup.

MANAGING YOUR ENERGY

Science has taught us that we can slice and dice the minutes of the day as efficiently as possible, but it's all for nothing if we don't have the same energy for meaningful dialogue during meetings on the back end of the day. That's why

....

Carving out moments in the day to recharge is neither a gift nor a luxury; it's a necessity.

....

actively managing our *energy* is far more important than managing our *time*.

Energy can be renewed by putting in place little bunkers in time where we can transition into a calmer state. This allows our parasympathetic nervous system to work its magic. Given the demands we face, these moments won't manifest out of thin air, which is where the discipline comes in.

Proactively managing our energy involves a disciplined approach to replenishing our reserves by defining the nonnegotiables we need in place. I know that's a tall order given our crazy schedules! Here are seven strategies to help you consistently put your best foot forward.

Strategy 1: The Power of Sleep

We all know that getting adequate sleep improves how we feel. But did you know it also enhances your emotional outlook, your ability to concentrate, your critical thinking skills, and your body's ability to repair itself? Heck, it even boosts your sex drive and helps prevent cardiovascular disease and diabetes.[9] This is one area you simply can't ignore.

Interestingly, researchers have found that senior executives tend to clock more hours of sleep time.[10] Why? Perhaps, as their careers progressed, they learned firsthand the importance of getting enough rest and its impact on their ability to lead effectively.

Athletes are no different. Tennis star Daniel Nestor

9 See Julia Rodriguez, "Sufficient Sleep Improves Libido in Women," Advanced Sleep Medicine Services, https://www.sleepdr.com/the-sleep-blog/sufficient-sleep -improves-libido-in-women/; "Why You Need to Get Enough Sleep for a Healthy Heart," Cleveland Clinic, November 2, 2020, https://health.clevelandclinic.org/for -a-healthy-heart-get-enough-sleep/; and Jennifer Purdie, "How Does Diabetes Affect Sleep?," Healthline, August 3, 2021, https://www.healthline.com/health/diabetes /diabetes-and-sleep.

10 Rasmus Hougaard and Jacqueline Carter, "Senior Executives Get More Sleep Than Everyone Else," *Harvard Business Review*, February 28, 2018, https://hbr .org/2018/02/senior-executives-get-more-sleep-than-everyone-else.

counts adequate sleep among the most crucial elements of his game. "I really struggled with getting enough sleep when traveling for games. Wimbledon in particular was a problem, so I learned to manage my day around it. I would go to bed thirteen hours ahead of when I needed to wake up, just to make sure I got a minimum of seven. That way, even if I didn't fall asleep right away, it wasn't a big deal."

Some tips?

- Start working through that stack of books you have on your night table! Reading a book before bed has been shown to improve sleep by up to 22 percent.[11]

- Recognize signs of fatigue, and call it out when lack of sleep is an issue. By being aware of the problem, we can more actively identify a solution.

- Create at least a thirty-minute window between work and sleep, giving the brain a chance to disengage.

- Practice meditation for a few minutes before bedtime to quiet your thoughts and decrease the likelihood of rumination.

- When you struggle to stay asleep, get out of bed

---

11 E. Finucane et al., "Does Reading a Book in Bed Make a Difference to Sleep in Comparison to Not Reading a Book in Bed? The People's Trial—an Online, Pragmatic, Randomised Trial," *Trials* 22, no. 1 (December 4, 2021): 873.

and move if you find yourself lying there for more than twenty minutes. This can relax your mind from distracting thoughts and avoid the brain associating sleep time with rumination.

- Download sleep apps that can help distract the mind to get back to catching some Zs.
- Ask your physician for recommendations on a personalized approach to getting some more rest.

By analyzing our habits and figuring out what works best, we can set up a regime that ensures we wake up refreshed and ready to go, repeatedly.

Strategy 2: Take a Breath

Breathing may be automatic, but we aren't automatically breathing in a way that serves us best. When we

....

By analyzing our habits and figuring out what works best, we can set up a regime that ensures we wake up refreshed and ready to go, repeatedly.

....

are stressed, our breathing shifts into a shallow and rapid pattern, preparing for the potential need to fight or flee. This leads to less fresh oxygen going to the body and brain, resulting in lower-quality thinking and higher levels of anxiety.[12] Double whammy.

Fill your lungs with some good old-fashioned oxygen, and you'll feel more present, engaged, and alert almost immediately. Not only that, but it benefits your cardiovascular health, nervous system, and mental well-being.[13] Navy SEALs reap these benefits by implementing "box breathing" in high-pressure situations.[14] That's a good tool to have in our back pocket when we need it most. Inhale for four seconds, hold it for four seconds, exhale for four seconds, and then hold that for four seconds. As you do this over and over, your concentration sharpens, and calm descends.

---

12 See "Rhythm of Breathing Affects Memory and Fear," Neuroscience News, December 7, 2016, https://neurosciencenews.com/memory-fear-breathing-5699/; and Kira M. Newman, "Is the Way You Breathe Making You Anxious?," Greater Good Magazine, November 10, 2020, https://greatergood.berkeley.edu/article/item/is_the_way_you_breathe_making_you_anxious.

13 Marc A. Russo, Danielle M. Santarelli, and Dean O'Rourke, "The Physiological Effects of Slow Breathing in the Healthy Human," *Breathe* 13, no. 4 (December 2017): 298–309, https://www.ncbi.nlm.nih.gov/pmc/articles/PMC5709795/.

14 Karthik Kumar, "Why Do Navy SEALs Use Box Breathing?," MedicineNet, November 18, 2021, https://www.medicinenet.com/why_do_navy_seals_use_box_breathing/article.htm.

Strategy 3: You Are What You Eat

The benefits of healthy food for our bodies are well known, but only now are we becoming aware of their significant impact on performance. One study found unhealthy diets can cut productivity by as much as 20 percent.[15] In the spirit of "grabbing something quickly," we tend to eat food that causes energy crashes in the middle of the day, decreasing our overall effectiveness.

Often, we think of the brain and body as two separate entities, but they are connected in every way. What we put into our bodies has an impact not only on how we feel but also on how the brain operates. The problem is, when stressed, we are prone to emotional eating,[16] and rather than putting something into the body that will decrease stress and increase productivity, we quickly find ourselves speed-dialing for a pizza.

Given its importance to our overall success, healthy eating is one area we really need to proactively set and

---

15 "Poor Workplace Nutrition Hits Workers' Health and Productivity, Says New ILO Report," International Labour Organization, September 15, 2005, https://www .ilo.org/global/about-the-ilo/newsroom/news/WCMS_005175/lang--en/index.htm.

16 "Work Burnout Tied to 'Emotional Eating' in Women: Study," Reuters, March 12, 2012, https://www.reuters.com/article/us-burnout/work-burnout-tied-to -emotional-eating-in-women-study-idUSBRE82C03G20120313.

forget—this is where habits are helpful. A few tactics the experts recommend include

- ensuring we have healthy snacks within reach.

- drawing up a basic meal plan so we can shop effectively and have easy go-to options.

- choosing the healthy (or the least unhealthy) option on the menu before arriving at a restaurant.

- engaging a meal delivery service to eliminate the need to worry about having healthy meals on hand.

Living a life of mastery is simply impossible if we're not refueling our bodies with the nutrients and energy they need to run like a well-oiled machine.

Strategy 4: Moments of Meditation

I promised at the outset of this chapter that by recharging I didn't mean candles and chanting, and I'm sticking to it. Meditation doesn't need to fit only into the category of pseudoscientific practices. It is, in fact, a research-backed approach to activate your parasympathetic nervous system and give your brain and body time to rest and rebuild.[17]

Find moments in the day when you can simply sit and close your eyes, looking inward. Meditation can quite literally create lasting change in a matter of weeks. A recent meta-analysis of twenty studies on meditation found that consistent practice for two months not only enhanced overall mood but also optimized the brain by altering the regions related to memory, learning, cognitive skills, emotional control, and awareness.[18] Talk about putting yourself into a position for high performance!

Strategy 5: Putting Gratitude in Our Attitude

Gratitude colors everything we experience and brings long-lasting positivity to how we interpret the world. It primes the brain to see possibilities rather than merely obstacles, opening us up to new ideas, new insights, and new levels of optimism. A fascinating study found that fundraisers who were primed with a pep talk from the director on how grateful she was for their engagement

17 Kieran C. R. Fox et al., "Is Meditation Associated with Altered Brain Structure? A Systematic Review and Meta-Analysis of Morphometric Neuroimaging in Meditation Practitioners," *Neuroscience and Biobehavioral Reviews* 43 (June 2014): 48–73, https://pubmed.ncbi.nlm.nih.gov/24705269/.

18 B. K. Hölzel et al., "Mindfulness Practice Leads to Increases in Regional Brain Gray Matter Density," *Psychiatry Research Journal* 191, no. 1 (January 30, 2011): 36–43.

made 50 percent more fundraising calls than their counterparts.[19] In another study, those who wrote about things they were grateful for continued to enjoy the benefits of optimism and better mental health twelve weeks after the practice ended.[20]

We naturally tend to gravitate toward what's wrong or what's missing. Balancing this natural tendency has massive benefits; where there is gratitude, happiness and calm will follow.

Strategy 6: Let's Take This Outside

Just as our office space doesn't always mean a desk and four walls, a meeting doesn't have to mean stale air under fluorescent lighting. Have a one-on-one meeting? Take the conversation outside and get up to speed while on a walk around the block. Have a short break in the day? One study found that undergraduate students who took fifteen-minute breaks outside scored

19 Adam M. Grant and Francesca Gino, "A Little Thanks Goes a Long Way: Explaining Why Gratitude Expressions Motivate Prosocial Behavior," *Journal of Personality and Social Psychology* 98, no. 6 (2010): 946–55, https://www.umkc.edu/facultyombuds /documents/grant_gino_jpsp_2010.pdf.

20 Y. Joel Wong et al., "Does Gratitude Writing Improve the Mental Health of Psychotherapy Clients? Evidence from a Randomized Controlled Trial," *Psychotherapy Research* 28, no. 2 (March 2018): 192–202, https://pubmed.ncbi.nlm.nih .gov/27139595/.

significantly higher on a subsequent focus assessment than those who stayed indoors.[21] We might also take the opportunity to get in a few minutes of breathing (fresh air!) and focus on all that we're grateful for too.

Fresh ideas often come with a shift away from directly focusing on the problem as the brain makes connections that weren't immediately obvious to the conscious mind. When a solution to a problem is eluding us, we need to stop banging our head against a keyboard and pound the pavement instead. The solution will likely surface, making the problem-solving process a literal walk in the park.

Strategy 7: Just Say No

As we saw in chapter 4, an occupational hazard of being an overachiever is that you chronically bite off more than you can chew. The calendar ends up being as packed as Miami beach during spring break.

---

21 Gerhard Blasche et al., "Comparison of Rest-Break Interventions during a Mentally Demanding Task," *Stress Health* 34, no. 5 (December 2018): 629–38, https://www.ncbi.nlm.nih.gov/pmc/articles/PMC6585675/.

OVERCOMING OVERWHELM

We can't control what people ask of us, but we can control what we take on. Setting boundaries and being choosy about what we say yes to is critical to high performance; otherwise, there isn't enough time to recharge, let alone get stuff done!

It's OK to be honest about why you can't take on a task. Maybe you're tired because you've already put in excessive hours that week, or perhaps you have conflicting obligations to family or simply have a plate that's already

---

When a solution to a problem is eluding us, we need to stop banging our head against a keyboard and pound the pavement instead.

---

full. If it's a priority, what else has to come off the calendar to make room for this new high-impact initiative or activity? If it's not a priority, how can you respectfully and effectively say no?

Many of us can relate to Wendy, the client I was telling you about earlier. We have seen firsthand how the expectations we place on ourselves can lead us to a constant fire-drill state as we run from one disaster to another. We tell ourselves that it will get better if we can just get through the next few weeks. But when we're playing a big game, the intensity doesn't abate or pause, waiting for us to catch up. The waves of work will keep rolling in. Rather than *waiting* for the breaks, we need to *create* them.

After John left home, Wendy realized it was time to make some serious adjustments. With her new vision in mind, she immediately sprang into action,

....

The waves of work will keep rolling in. Rather than waiting for the breaks, we need to create them.

....

building a blueprint for her life that would allow her to be present and grounded and feeling her best. The plan included taking a cell phone–free walk with her dogs in the morning, carving out room to fit exercise back into her schedule, and creating time for lunches with friends once a month, tech-free. She even signed up for guitar lessons to exercise a different part of her brain and get back to one of her favorite hobbies.

Wendy took John out for dinner to share her new plan and asked if he would give their marriage another chance. He moved back in, and the benefits of her incremental changes started paying off. Not only did she and John rekindle and rebuild their love life, but her engagement at work was less reactive and scattered.

Yes, she had a lot on her plate, and no, her job didn't allow for much downtime. But therein lies the paradox: the moment you feel that you can't take a break is often when you need one the most.

DEEPENING THE WORK

KEY TAKEAWAYS

- Physical and mental depletion manifest in errors, loss of concentration, mood swings, and sleeplessness. These symptoms can affect productivity, performance, and relationships.

- Being disciplined when it comes to rest will make you more successful.

- Recharging requires you to make choices throughout the day to slow down, even if only for a moment.

- Think about the practices you need to maintain to feel energized and able to perform at your best all day.

- Keep in mind the seven strategies for caring for yourself and bringing out your best: sleep, taking breaks, meditation, gratitude, slowing down, nutrition, and saying no.

- Wendy's story is a testament that you can make meaningful changes to take back control of your life and mend broken relationships.

- Remember to prioritize yourself before you widen your circle and begin to care for others. As Richard Branson reminds us, "You need to get yourself in order first."

EXPLORATORY QUESTIONS

- Make a list of all the things that energize you. What do you notice?

- Make a list of all the things that drain your energy. What do you notice?

- If you had more time for yourself, what would you do with it?

TASKS

1. Not all stress is created equal. Yerkes-Dobson law proposes that stress impacts performance in various ways, with moderate stress enhancing performance, and overly high levels of stress decreasing performance. Look for moments when you feel a healthy dose of stress and when you feel pushed over the edge into being strained.

2. Make a list of tactics you can employ to bring down the level of stress when it has spiked into an unhealthy and unproductive level. Determine what works best for you.

Chapter 12

MAKING TIME
TO DANCE IN THE RAIN

I will just create, and if it works, it works, and if it
doesn't, I'll create something else. I don't have any
limitations on what I think I could do or be.

—OPRAH WINFREY, TALK SHOW HOST, TELEVISION
PRODUCER, ACTRESS, AUTHOR, AND PHILANTHROPIST

FOR ME, BRAIN science is personal.

I opened this book with the story of our confrontation with a man wielding a knife. Now that we've reached the book's closing pages, I want to share something a little more intimate.

Long before those terrible moments in the car with my kids, my family and I were confronted by a different challenge. One that triggered an even greater sense of jeopardy and ignited a lifelong passion to study the brain. It started the moment our son stopped breathing.

At three-years old, our son, whom I affectionately call Bear, fell victim to a rare condition where his brain would suddenly stop sending the signal to his lungs to breathe. We would see him gasping for air, eyes wide with a look of sheer terror, before turning blue and falling to the floor unconscious. The first time it happened, we thought we had lost him. My husband scooped him up and ran outside, screaming for help, with this small, seemingly lifeless body bouncing around in his arms. That's not a memory I will easily forget.

Over the following five years, his condition evolved, threatening to take his life on more than one occasion. I read voraciously about the brain, desperately seeking that one elusive nugget the doctors might be missing, as I scrolled through research papers and medical journals all night until falling asleep at my desk. Because of the rarity of his condition, I struggled to find any meaningful information to lean on. As a family, we were left without answers.

By the time he was eight years old, we were still in and out of hospitals, emotionally drained and physically exhausted. My husband and I took the kids up to the mountains for the weekend to have a reprieve from the intensity of it all. While playing board games around the kitchen table, watching the rain coming down outside, my son asked to go out for a walk. The eagerness in his tone was palpable, so I obliged. He and I put on our raincoats and headed out to brave the weather.

About five hundred feet from our condo, he stopped, looked up at the sky, stretched out his arms, and just started spinning. His smile grew bigger and bigger as the rain fell on his face. Soon he was pulling off his raincoat and then his T-shirt, letting the cold rain pelt down on his bare chest. I urged him to put his coat back on, telling him that it was time to go back inside—but any instinct I had quickly dissipated when he looked up at me with his sweet little smile and said, "Mom, what if I never get to do this again?"

My husband, who had been watching from the window, seemed to intuitively understand the importance of the moment and came running down with my daughter in tow. By the time they reached us, he, too, had taken off his shirt, and there they were, the three of them, bouncing around, splashing in puddles, enjoying the magic of the moment.

CHOOSING GREATNESS

The silver lining of it all is that my children grew up with an intimate understanding of life's incredible fragility. Although the reasons for this understanding may be painful, they are highly in tune with the awe and wonder of the world, finding their way to shine despite the rainfall they have weathered. And I am grateful to say that after years of hardship, with the right medical team, hard work, and an optimistic outlook, our son is now healthy and thriving. Any remnants of his illness are nothing more than memories, challenges he has finally left behind.

Yes, we as a family have endured a great deal of grief, fear, and worry. But the more I share this story, the more I realize that all of us have weathered our own storms. In the moment, these experiences might weigh us down. Pull us under. But once we catch our breath and find our footing, they have the power to propel us forward with an even greater sense of perspective and intensity.

Because we are still here.

We are still standing.

And I'm not done living yet.

Let's use our energy and efforts to keep on growing. Leaning into the discomfort that comes with choosing growth, sharpening the skills that will lead us to the life we want to be living. With growth, there is no shortage of opportunities to reach for or achievements to run toward. Each time we stretch, regardless of the outcome, we are strengthening and expanding our capabilities and perspectives, positioning ourselves for long-term success.

I know that may sound Pollyannaish, but you'll notice I never said the word *easy*. Our dreams won't

> **With growth, there is no shortage of opportunities to reach for or achievements to run toward.**

unfold with the same ease as online shopping. We can't just conjure up our ideal future, put it in our shopping cart, and wait for it to arrive at the front door.

Instead, we need to consciously expand that moment between an event and our reaction to it and choose the behavior or thought that will accelerate our progress. Discomfort be damned. Choose. And if you hit a setback, choose again. In the words of Richard Branson, "Screw it. Just do it!" Step out of the daily stream of tasks to identify the activities that have the highest possible return, moving you toward your own version of Greatness. Surround yourself with people who can put more spring in your step, more mojo in the tank, more meaning in every moment. Through it all, remember to communicate in a connected, credible, and compelling way while honoring your biology and respecting its limits.

Growth is a lifelong experience. That's why this book is intended to be a lifelong companion. Come back to it like you would an old friend who will give you a nudge when you need it the most—an old friend who can help you step back and think about the areas of your life where you are playing too small or playing it too safe, so you can push yourself one step further, climb up one step higher, and make the choices that will have the greatest impact every step along the way.

Let's face it. There will come a day when the music stops playing, maybe even without warning. But every moment between now and then is just waiting to be filled with your song.

Choose the music you want to be making.

And don't forget to dance in the rain.

CHOOSING GREATNESS
ADDITIONAL RESOURCES

If you want to continue learning more to master the skills that will launch your career exponentially forward, we have several resources available:

Livestream Programs
Christina facilitates several livestream programs to accelerate results for you, your team, and the business. These programs include Public Speaking Mastery, Leadership Excellence, High-Impact Communication, and more. Register and save your seat today at curtisleadership.com.

Executive Coaching Programs
Executive coaching delivers breakthrough results by arming leaders with data-driven, personalized strategies. Walk away with the tactics, tools, and frameworks you need to drive rapid growth in the areas you need it most. Reach out to Christina and her team to learn more about our executive coaching programs at curtisleadership.com.

High-Performance Team Programs
What would your team be capable of achieving if they transformed into a high-performance team? High-performance teams outperform their counterparts 3 to 1, experiencing 72 percent less stress, 106 percent more energy, and 42 percent lower burnout. Why? They lean on one another and consistently show up with high levels of innovation and accountability. Register your team today for a workshop at curtiseladership.com.

360 Feedback Reviews
Gather the data required to assess strengths and opportunities at an individual, team, or department level. Curtis Leadership has access to world-class tools including the Hogan® assessment, Five Behaviors of a Team® assessment, DiSC® assessment, and 360 Feedback assessment, to you get the data you need to make highly informed decisions.

ADDITIONAL RESOURCES

Podcasts and Articles
Christina is a thought leader on motivation and goal attainment who has articles published in *Harvard Business Review*, *Psychology Today*, and *Forbes* magazine. She has also been interviewed on several podcasts. To learn more, check out the Featured In section at curtis-leadership.com.

Further Recommended Reading
Interested in some of my favorite reads? Here's a list of the top ten I recommend!

- **The Happiness Advantage: How a Positive Brain Fuels Success in Work and Life**, by Shawn Achor

- **Drive: The Surprising Truth About What Motivates Us**, by Daniel H. Pink

- **The Confidence Code: The Science and Art of Self-Assurance: What Women Should Know**, by Katty Kay and Claire Shipman

- **Executive Presence: The Missing Link Between Merit and Success**, by Sylvia Ann Hewlett

- **Quiet: The Power of Introverts in a World That Can't Stop Talking**, by Susan Cain, Kathe Mazur, et al.

- **Spark: The Revolutionary New Science of Exercise and the Brain**, by John J. Ratey and Eric Hagerman

- **Daring Greatly: How the Courage to Be Vulnerable Transforms the Way We Live, Love, Parent, and Lead**, by Brené Brown

- **The Obstacle Is the Way: The Timeless Art of Turning Trials into Triumph,** by Ryan Holiday

- **Grit: The Power of Passion and Perseverance**, by Angela Duckworth

- **Building a StoryBrand: Clarify Your Message So Customers Will Listen,** by Donald Miller

ACKNOWLEDGMENTS

....

CHOOSING GREATNESS was a team effort, and I am immeasurably grateful to those who helped take this book across the goal line!

Thank you to my husband, who believed in the message and created the space in our lives to bring this book to life. Steven, thirty years of knowing you have made me a better parent, partner, and person.

Thank you to my children, who challenged me every day to live the book's principles. Watching you courageously form your own perspectives and show up as such powerful and purposeful young adults has been the greatest thrill of my life. Never forget the lessons you continue to teach me and others—be you, choose happiness, and love deeply—to the moon and back.

ACKNOWLEDGMENTS

To my mom, dad, and Jason and Liz, for enduring the years of worry and wonder as I searched to find myself as a person: there isn't a day that goes by without me counting my blessings to have you as friends and mentors. Thank you, Ellen and John, for your constant support, and Laura and Aaron for showing me what excellence looks like. I am a better person for being able to call each of you, my family.

Thank you to the amazing women in my circle. I have limitless admiration, respect, and love for who you are as people and how you unapologetically show up and make waves in this world!

I want to thank my editor, Graham Verdon, for his partnership throughout. I couldn't have written a book without your direction and gentle nudges. To Billie Brownell, who endured countless tweaks in the manuscript and had patience with me through the process. Thank you to Jennifer Gingerich, Justin Batt, and Lauren Ward for pushing this project forward and shaping the book into what it is today. Thank you to Bruce Gore for the beautiful cover, Mary Susan Oleson for the interior design, and Denise Zimmermann for her sketches. And

ACKNOWLEDGMENTS

thank you to the team at Simon & Schuster for getting this book into the hands of readers!

Finally, to all the voices whom I captured in conversations over the years. Richard Branson, Jonathan Johnson, Daniel Nestor, Lara Merriken, Teena Piccione, Kim Rivera, Javier Rodriguez, Eric Severson, Everett Thomas, and Phyllis Yale—thank you for sharing your insights and supporting me in this endeavor. Each of you took the time to enhance and sharpen the choices of others as they find their own path to Greatness. For that, I am eternally grateful.

ABOUT THE AUTHOR

CHRISTINA CURTIS is the Founder of Curtis Leadership Consulting, a boutique firm supporting world-class entrepreneurs and Fortune 500 executives. A thought leader on motivation and goal attainment, Christina's work has been featured in *Harvard Business Review*, *Forbes*, *Entrepreneur*, *Fortune*, and *Psychology Today*. Christina is an accredited Master Coach—a designation held by less than 2 percent of business coaches worldwide—and earned her master's degree in organizational psychology from the University of London and a bachelor of arts (honors) degree from Queens University in Canada. She is a certified NeuroLeadership specialist.

www.curtisleadership.com
LinkedIn: www.linkedin.com/in/christinacurtisofficial
Instagram: @christinacurtisofficial
Twitter: @curtis_coaching